God My Keeper

Joy in His Daily Doses of Grace

A BREAST CANCER JOURNEY OF FAITH, HOPE AND HEALING

Bro. & Sis Billups!

Thank you and God bless you for your many prayers, for the wonderful cards you sent my way over the months and for exhibited acts of Christian Love! I thank God for you and your friendship & Love! God had blessed me to Remission and there

Donna Joy Pearson

is a Reason for this season and I will give Him the glory. He was the Author of this book I only penned it, as He blessed me with daily doses of grace, on my journey. He said, "write, so others will know" and I did. Enjoy & share!
All for Him!
Donna Jan 6, 2008

All Scripture references are from The King James Version, Copyright 1989 Thomas Nelson, Inc

ISBN: 978-1-60383-030-0

Published by:
Holy Fire Publishing
Unit 116
1525-D Old Trolley Rd.
Summerville, SC 29485

www.ChristianPublish.com

Cover Design: Jay Cookingham

Printed in the United States of America and the United Kingdom

Dedication

Life's special people have left indelible marks in my heart. This writing is dedicated to the loving memory of my parents, **Homer E. Kelly, Sr.**, who fought a gallant battle with lung cancer, even to remission, and my dear mother, **Faye**, (dad's nurse and angel of encouragement). Also, to the unforgettable memory of my **Sissy**, who gave her all in the journey and yet always remained positive; and lastly as a memorial honorarium to my neighbor **"Fly"** who lost his battle with lung cancer. His smile, his wave and "howdy neighbor" goodness is greatly missed!

Acknowledgements

There are so many people I need to thank. I'll begin with my family: my husband, Sam (my helpmate and the love of my life), my daughters, Holly and Kellee (the VERY best) and Son's-in-law, Matt and Steve; my brothers, Gene, Danny, Freddie and Kelvin; and so many faithful and loving friends.

Thank you to great doctors and nurses; prayer warriors and pastors of our church connections near and far.

I give God thanks for one and all (for every prayer, phone call, visit, card, email and gift of encouragement).

You have all played a major role in the success of this unforgettable journey. I CALL YOU FRIENDS! I AM BLESSED BEYOND MEASURE!

Contents

Foreword

A cancer journey (no matter what kind) is one that none of us would ever choose but one that can teach many lessons of "grace". *"To everything there is a season"* and "reason" *"a time to every purpose under the heaven"*. (Ecclesiastes 3:1)

For almost 15 years I have aspired of writing two books (one of my childhood memories and the other, a children's book about Heaven). Over these years I've compiled a collection of thoughts, memories and ideas; thinking when I retired, I would get started.

God changed my mind! He "allowed" me to be taken from the busy-ness of church ministry to the "business" of pen and ink! He has shown me, by His grace, how I might be a minister of that grace to others on the breast cancer journey.

God has "poured" His grace into me, daily! I haven't <u>earned</u> His grace, but I have <u>learned</u> more of it! God's pouring grace into me brought back memories of mother's Castor Oil. She could just look into my eyes or say *"Stick out your tongue"* and she'd declare my <u>need</u> for a dose. Then, she'd "pour" it in me! I sure didn't like it, (YUK!); but it served its purpose. I was the "apple" of my mother's eye and she wanted my body well. God's daily doses of grace are confirmation that He *"kept me as the apple of His eye"* (Psalm 17:8). He KNEW when I needed grace and I <u>loved</u> every dose (YUM!). He wanted my spirit well. God's grace IS good! "Open up" and enjoy these daily doses!

O Lord, thou hast searched me, and knoweth me. Thou knowest my downsitting and mine uprising, thou understandest my thought afar off. Thou compassest my path and my lying down and art acquainted with all my ways. For there is not a word in my tongue, but, lo, O Lord, thou knowest it altogether.

Psalm 139:1-4

"Diagnosis – the 'C' Word"

Daily Dose of Grace:
When you are weak, He makes you strong

"........................, the race is not to the swift, nor the battle to the strong, neither yet bread to the wise, nor yet riches to men of understanding, nor yet favour to men of skill; but time and chance happeneth to them all. For man also knoweth not his time: as the fishes that are taken in an evil net, and as the birds that are caught in the snares; so are the sons of men snared in an evil time, when it falleth suddenly upon them."
Ecclesiastes 9:11-12

I had been 13 years cancer free. I didn't want to hear that "C" word again! September, 1993 was my first cancer diagnosis. I'll never forget that day! I was at the office and my gynecologist called. He said, "Can you come by the office, we need to talk about your test results?" The big "C" word never crossed my mind! I'm thinking "hormones" or "change of life". I was early into my 40's and just like the pain of childbirth, the change of life was the inevitable; (thank you Eve!). I had witnessed too, many women in the church choir turn flush red and grab fans and tissues; and I would chuckle and think, "How can a hot flash be so bad?" I WISH the doctor HAD told me, on that day, my presumption was right; but it wasn't! His diagnosis and prognosis put me into a state of shock and disbelief! I "knew the truth, but didn't want to". As Solomon said, *"but time and chance happeneth to them all"*. (Eccl. 9:11)

Again on December 7, 2006, I knew the truth but didn't want to! NO ONE wants to hear "breast cancer"! Cancer is one of the most prominent, dreaded and suspected diseases known in this country. With every medical problem and test, we all fret that it could be the "C" word. Solomon said, *"For man also knoweth not his time:..............so are the sons of men snared in an evil time, when it falleth suddenly upon them."* Eccl. 9:12. Cancer, disease, heartbreak, pain and suffering are all traps of the devil and they all come "suddenly". God does not cause any snares to fall upon us. If we call him Father He is our Protector and Healer. He is Almighty and All Powerful and may "allow" us to go through some of these things to build our faith, to draw us closer to Him, to exemplify Him, and PERHAPS even to acknowledge that He is GOD!!

Times are evil and Satan is still alive and well, *"Seeking whom he may devour"*. Like the Apostle Paul said of his "thorn in the flesh", *"I take pleasure in infirmities, reproaches, necessities, persecutions and distresses FOR CHRIST'S SAKE: for when I am weak then I am strong"* II Cor. 12:10. Cancer did not befall me because of my *strength (battle to the strong)* or my *speed (race to the swift)*, Eccl 9:11, but that I might be an example of a great faith and the measureless mercy of a loving God! I will not succumb to this thorn in my flesh as the devil would desire! Some days are hard, some nights are long but with God's hand in mine I won't run this race alone. *"Nevertheless I am with thee; thou hast holden me by my right hand."* Psalm 73:23.

If you ever hear the word: cancer, "know the truth and don't want to", you can grow in a GREAT faith and experience the MEASURELESS mercy of a God who really does love you and will be your Guide in the journey.

"I Am Not, Helpless, Hopeless or Powerless"

Daily Dose of Grace:
God's work in you, will be completed

"For the kingdom of God is not meat and drink; but righteousness, and peace, and joy in the Holy Ghost"
Romans 14:17-18

Today I went to church and my Pastor's sermon was RIGHT ON! Just what I needed! It put a spirit to persevere in me! God gave me peace because I am His, He OWNS me! Cancer has attacked my body but it <u>does not</u> own me! I can even feel "invincible". God's presence makes it possible! *"Being confident of this very thing, that he which hath begun a good work in you will perform it until the day of Jesus Christ;"* (Phil. 1:6).

Today I have no fear because 1) *"Where the spirit of the Lord is, there is liberty"* (II Cor. 3:17). His Spirit lives <u>within</u> me! 2) He has filled my life with *"righteousness, peace and joy in the Holy Spirit"* (Rom 14:17). His peace, joy and righteousness are so abundant there is no room for fear, helplessness, hopelessness or powerlessness! 3) *"My hope is in knowing that He began a good work in me and will complete it"*. 4) My "power" comes from Him; it may require my patience in waiting but <u>power</u> is in His promise and I am determined, (Luke 24:49). 5) If a battle is necessary, I am not helpless; I will remain "strong" in Him and the power of His might". I'll go forth in full armor and withstand! I have no fear because I know the Captain! 6) I will remain at "His right hand" and will not be forgotten, (Acts 2:34). He knows and cares! **My God is Powerful!**

"He Holds me Up, I Look Up"

Daily Dose of Grace:
Remain cheerful, never doubt, and never fear

"And immediately Jesus stretched forth his hand and caught him, and said unto him, O thou of little faith, wherefore didst thou doubt?
Matthew 14:31

Some days I worry about how tough this trip might be and wonder if I will make it! I have always loved this story in Matthew! Jesus words, *"Be of good cheer, it is I, be not afraid"*, give me such great hope! I'm glad God loves me and is always available to "hold me up". So many times I have heard sermons preached on this passage of Scripture. Winds and storms <u>will</u> come our way in life; sometimes "boisterous" winds come. We may be afraid and we may start to lose hope but our God is always near and available to "hold us up"!

 You've heard about the storms of life and you believe in God's presence, but until you find yourself truly **in the midst of the storm**, you will never know **the strength of your faith!**

Cancer has brought a boisterous storm my direction but God has thrown out the life-line. I will look up and grab it, I won't be afraid; He will save me from this storm! I love Matthew 14: 31.   Peter began to sink, looked up and saw Jesus was there to save Him! **My God is Ubiquitous!**

Thank you God for holding me up! Continue to give me the great faith to LOOK UP!

"Running Home"

Daily Dose of Grace:
God's greatness is unsearchable.

"Blessed be the Lord my strength………, my goodness, and my fortress; my high tower, and my deliverer; my shield,"
Psalm 144:1-2

God gives all of us <u>weapons</u> to fight the battles of life. I consider His Word my sword and faith my shield, but if I lay them down and surrender to the wars that come my way, my time is limited! *"God is my strength, He teaches my hands to war and my fingers to fight"* (Verse 1). I claim this verse as my HOPE in this battle! I have inventoried my weapons and sharpened my sword.

I will not surrender to the attacks of Satan! I have begun a third battle for good health. The devil continues to try to take me out or to cause my surrender but he will not win. ***"God is my Goodness, my Fortress, my High Tower, my Deliverer, and my Shield. In Him, I will put my trust."*** (Verse 2). I will not sit down; I will not surrender to the wiles of the devil! I will fight with a great faith! Today, Jan 22, 2007, I go to receive my orders, my map for the journey. My faith will remain positive and patience and strength will prevail as I *"Run for Home"*!

As in the old baseball terminology, I would rebuke the devil with these words, *"Three strikes you are out! A "Home Run" is within my reach, God is my Coach, the Referee of my life and He ALONE will make the call!*

"I Can Do This"

Daily Dose of Grace:
God will give you strength

"All the ways of a man are clean in his own eyes; but the Lord weigheth the spirit."
Proverbs 16:2

Today, February 5, 2007, I begin my "treatment" journey for breast cancer. God's will is that I believe in the possibility of healing and pursue with a purpose. God is my Healer, NOT my hurter! He has a purpose for my life and every year of my life is more exciting as He leads me in His way. His purpose was established at the moment of my conception, *"In my mother's womb He knew me."* (Psalm 139:15) I know God walks beside me, before me and behind me, to encourage me. In agreement with the words of the Apostle Paul, *"I will press toward the mark for the prize of the high calling of God in Christ Jesus."* (Philippians 3:14)

Proverbs 16:1 assures me that God prepares my heart, Verse 9 says, *"Man's heart devises a way"*, (I am human!) But God directs my steps! Because I trust and lean on Him, *"I can do this"*! I don't look forward to the days of sickness or the challenges that I may face, but God says, *"Lean on me – WE can do this!"* **My God is loving!**

God still has plans for me. My mind continues to work!

Ministry with children is over-flowing my brain – God gives me this promise, *"I can do all things through Christ who strengtheneth me"* (Phil. 4:13). He is also feeding my mind with thoughts of "good health" returning. God is showing me possibilities and I know with Him, *"I can do this"*!

"Keep Looking Up"

Daily Dose of Grace:
God will never leave you

"Jesus Christ the same yesterday, and today, and forever. Be not carried away with divers and strange doctrines, for it is a good thing that the heart be established with grace...."
Proverbs 13:8-9

On this 4th day after my first chemo treatment I am beginning to feel stronger. I prayed this morning, *"God, I just want to be my old self again, back to normal"*! When I grabbed my Bible and devotional guide, God put a new perk in my day! My devotional guide said, "Consider this day a new beginning, a fresh start"!

Before I started cancer treatments, my doctors and nurses told me, *"Things will come, things will go, some days good, some not so good"*. They encouraged me to take each day, one at a time and not to dwell on what tomorrow might be, at how others in chemo are affected or listen to consequences of others journey. They said, "Every person is different! How you are affected may not be the same as another person, even if he/she is on the same treatment plan." (Prov. 27:1) One thing I can boast of is that my God is *"the same yesterday, today and forever"* (Heb 13:8) and that *"He will never leave me or forsake me"* (Heb 13:15).

I have felt so bad this week; it is difficult to describe! God said to me, this morning, *"Don't look away,* (when I look "away" I'm ignoring God*); don't look down,* (when I look "down" I'm considering giving up) *keep looking up!* (When I look "up" I'm counting on God)." I have had to remind MYSELF of the message I gave to my family when I told them of the cancer diagnosis. I said, "I expect each of you to remain positive with me, keep looking up! If I see you, depressed or looking down, I will KICK you in the shin and you WILL look up!" So must I!

THANK YOU GOD FOR ALWAYS BEING BY MY SIDE! You are ever present!

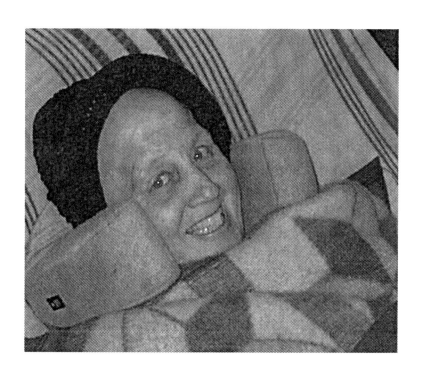

Thou hast beset me behind and before, and laid thine hand upon me. Such knowledge is too wonderful for me; it is too high, I cannot attain unto it. Whither shall I go from thy spirit? Or whither shall I flee from thy presence?
Psalm 139:5-7

"In Weakness, be Strong"

Daily Dose of Grace:
God will rock you in His arms

"Hear me, the Lord is with you while you are with Him and if you seek Him, He will be found."
II Chronicles 15:2

And the prayer of faith shall save the sick, and the Lord shall raise him up;.......(James 5:14)

Recent days have been a challenge. The weakness and sick feeling is laborious. My illness does not negate God's presence beside me. I remember last night, praying, "Lord hold me in Your arms, I want comfort and rest." I felt as if I was being "rocked in His arms". Just like Azariah said to Asa in II Chron. 15:2. If I stay close to Him, He will stay close to me (II Chron. 15: 4), *"But when they in their trouble did turn unto the Lord God of Israel and sought him, he was found of them."*

I have become somewhat depressed over the past week because I'm seeing the possibility of my SOON RETURN to ministry (on staff) as slim. I'm concerned that my connection from a distance is lacking. I am discouraged to think that plans I attribute to God's guidance will need to be put on hold. Is the dream for a thriving Children's Ministry at my church, now for naught? I know Satan would have me believe that it is so. Verse 7 is a great inspiration to me. It says, *"Be strong, let not your hands be weak, for your work will be rewarded."* That gives me hope that God still has plans for me <u>from a distance</u>. My ultimate prayer is that others in the church will step forward and carry on the business of a vibrant and promising Children's Ministry.

People should *"enter into covenant and seek God with all their souls"* (vs. 12). When that covenant is entered into whole-heartedly, God will give <u>me rest</u> (vs. 15). It is possible, without my physical presence, BUT priority needs to prevail. How important are the lives of children? My prayer is that people will "fall in love" and get a vision of the possibilities and the blessings!

God, I trust YOUR intervention! You are Providential!

Uncompromised Strength"

DAILY DOSE OF GRACE:
God gives strength to the soul that purges the tears

"Though I walk in the midst of trouble, He will revive me, stretch forth His hand to hold back the devil and save me with His right hand."
Psalm 138:7

In the past weeks, there have been times when I have taken steps forward and some day's steps backward. Sometimes the backward steps make me cry. In Psalm 138:3, David said, *"In the day when I cried, Thou (God) answered me, and strengthened me with strength in my soul."* Soul strength will purge the tears.

My tears would come as I would cry in desperation to God for added strength and courage. *"Though I walk in the midst of trouble, He will revive me, stretch forth His hand to hold back the devil and save me with His right hand"* (Psalm 138:7). I am so thankful to know He is right beside me, all the time!

When days come and tears fall, God's thoughts will always and forever outnumber the tears. David said in Psalm 139:17-18, *"How precious are your thoughts, Oh God, How great is the sum of them, they are more than the sand."* That's how I know **"Tears Do Not Compromise My Strength"**. Tears remind me of God's thoughts! I am ALWAYS on His mind!

"An Eye on the Prize"

Daily Dose of Grace:
God is your Pace-Setter and keeps you strong in heart

"Know ye not that they which run in a race run all, but one receiveth the prize? So run, that ye may obtain."
I Corinthians 9:24

The time came for my first follow-up appointment with my Oncologist, <u>after</u> my first chemo treatment. It was February 19, 2007! My first BIG hit (treatment) had been on Feb 5th. I had told my husband in the days prior that my doctor <u>had better</u> be able to give <u>just cause</u> that other treatments were necessary, because I was ready to QUIT! The after-affects were just too much. I didn't want to be THAT sick again or in the hospital (as I had been with pneumonia). Could my focus be on getting better and could I DEAL WITH the discomfort?

Our youngest daughter, Holly, went with me for the appointment. I know her dad must have informed her of my intentions, so she wanted to be with me, #1 to hear the doctor's defense and #2 to encourage me to make the <u>right</u> choice, to "hang in".

My heart was beginning to turn toward comfort and away from the focus of "healing". In Proverbs 4:23, Solomon said, *"Keep your heart with diligence for out of it are the issues of life."* I had allowed the devil to fool me into thinking that life wasn't as important as my comfort. My doctor helped me to see that there is good in some of the discomforts we must face in life! He told me he could only predict a 50 to 50 chance of my survival without treatment, versus a 95% chance with treatment. He said that the kind of cancer I had would be so aggressive and PAST the possibility of healing, if I did not pursue the full course of treatment. He convinced me that the COST (discomfort) would be worth the PRIZE (healing). I said, *"Let's do it!"* For a moment, Satan had drawn my eye from the prize and tempted my retreat!

God in His goodness points me to His Word spoken by the Apostle Paul to the church of Corinth in I Cor. 9:24. If I RUN now, yes, there will be some discomfort; but God has convinced me that this is the ideal route (path). With God as my pace-setter, I can think ONLY of winning! I will remain diligent and strong of heart in this race against cancer! **My God is invisible** to the human eye, but present in my heart!

I know God is my Healer; He has provided the route, the coach (my doctor), the cheerleaders (my family and friends), given me a new heart (the desire), and a "refocus" on the prize of healing! *Thank You, Father, for direction and provision of the path to the prize.* Now I can say with all sincerity, *"I press toward the mark......"* (Phil 3:14) My stride may be slow but will grow to swiftness as I *"Keep (MY) Eye on the Prize"*!

"The Power of the Human Spirit"

Daily Dose of Grace:
Jump in with spirit, encourage others

*"Let us therefore, follow after the things which make for peace, and
things wherewith one may edify another."*
Romans 14:19-21

I have always been a person who is extremely uncomfortable in an environment of conflict or storms. Most often I would just want to run away turn my head and leave it behind. I have done that at times in my life. I still have a reluctance to step in and try to "still the storms" because, like a lifeguard who jumps in to pull out a drowning person, there's always the distinct possibility that he will be pulled under by the floundering swimmer. I may delay because I don't want to get pulled under. So it was for me in the decision to DO or NOT TO DO chemo therapy. I wondered, "Would it be worth the chance, would I go under?"

God's dose of grace today told me that my spirit should be positive! I should have such a peaceful and encouraging spirit about me that it, in itself, can affect the spirit of others and give them hope. Like the lifeguard; he MUST have a powerful "will" to JUMP IN for the sake of a drowning swimmer. What hope would there be for him, otherwise? I am going to JUMP IN to this chemo-therapy with a spirit of hope and determination and through the power of human spirit, fed by the power of the Holy Spirit, I will live to EDIFY, to "LIFT UP" others who may be drowning!

"All for Him"

Daily Dose of Grace:
Make known the JOY of your faith

*"Whether therefore ye eat, or drink, or whatsoever ye do, do all to
the glory of God."*
I Corinthians 10:31

I've discovered over the years that I have an innate ability to
"read" people, when I take time to really observe them. It's
hard to fool me! I can tell when there's real love; I can see
when there is real compassion, and I can see hurt and
confusion AND the mediocre. I am a real people watcher! I
can see attitudes, I can see care! And, over the weeks,
watching people and their reaction to me (my frailness,
paleness, slowness and weakness, etc.) has caused me to be
more aware that they see a difference in me. To them I may
not look like the same person, but I am! Not only that, but
most of them really do not know how to "respond" to me. I
said in the beginning I did not want "pity" but "prayer"! I
just hope that they can see me "inside" and overlook the
outward appearance. What do they see "in" me?

My LIFE VERSE for years has been I Cor. 10:31. From this
verse, I penned my salutation, *"All for Him"*. I want all I do,
all people see of me, even in these days, to honor God. I am
not perfect, the perfect patient or example but I certainly
strive to please Him and to remain pleasing in His sight!
When I stumble, when I am weak, He picks me up, gives me a
hug and gives me added strength for the journey. I'm

confident that He'll return me to "serve", "to give all" in His name and I continue to give thanks to Him. (Col 3:22).

I long for people to SEE THE JOY I have in my faith! I want them to see my faith in ACTION and never wonder or doubt that all I long for in this life is to be ALL FOR HIM, ALL THE TIME! One day I will receive a just reward for serving the Lord. (Col 3:24) There just can't be anything better than living "ALL FOR HIM"!!

"Random Acts of Love"

Daily Dose of Grace:
Loving relationships require attention, compassion, and connection

"Keep yourself in love.......look for mercy in the Lord Jesus Christ."
Jude 20-22

God, I am so thankful You choose to love me! Some days I feel forgotten (alone) on this journey and wonder *"Where is mercy and love? Boy, I could really use a "friend" today!"* Love is a choice to be made. God commands it but does not force it on us. We choose to have a relationship with God (to know Him) and I John 4:7-8 tells us that when we know God we will know how to love in return; *"Love is of God and everyone that loveth is born of God and knoweth God."* God will give us eyes of mercy and compassion. We have become a society of "apathy" and "busy-ness" that has hindered random acts of love.

I honestly believe that many people have such a FEAR of the word CANCER that when they hear it, they automatically think "death" and they avoid confrontation with it and sadly miss connection with people who are dealing with it. It, almost makes the stricken feel "contagious" or as a leper! I see a GREAT need for people to "know" how to relate through "Random Acts of Kindness". FEAR blocks a much needed LOVE connection.

Ina, (my Kentucky Mom) came to see me today, delivering a random act of kindness my way! She has been strength and encouragement to me in two other battles I've faced. She doesn't "pity" me she "supports" me! I admire exhibited love. It isn't costly; it is a random act such as a smile, a touch, a prayer, a phone call, or a visit. Random acts are not obligatory but are driven by love.

"Lord, help me to love, through it all! No matter the pain, the sickness, loneliness and disappointments in the days ahead, may others see "love" abounding and obvious in me. May 'Random Acts of Love' and teaching others how to, be MY passion! I will not feel obligated, but blessed to share Your love". *"If we love one another, His love is perfected in us and He dwells in us."* (I John 4:12)

"A Mind Set on Good Thoughts"

Daily Dose of Grace:
God's mind is always on me

"Set your affection on things above, not on things on the earth."
Colossians 3:2

Over the past weeks I have had people say to me, *"You have such great faith."*, and *"You have such a great attitude"*; *"Thanks for being such a great encourager, when "we" should be encouraging you."* Because *"My life is hid with Christ, in God"* (Col. 3:3), I can focus on good thoughts because *"Christ is my life"* (Col. 3:4).

I have hope in the possibility of a return to good health! I want people to see that hope in me! I long to live for Christ and be a <u>positive</u> influence so others may see HIM in me, even through any difficult and challenging times. I do not want my "faith" to be a SHOW for the attention of others (for my glory) but ALL for God!!

Should my mind-set and my faith in the weeks ahead lead ONE lost soul to faith in Jesus Christ or give ONE cancer ridden person "hope"; I will give God the praise for the opportunity to *"Set my mind on good thoughts"*. To God be all glory and praise! *"I will keep Him in perfect peace; His mind is stayed on me"*. (Isaiah 26:3)

"A Vision of Faith - A Hope to Dream"

Daily Dose of Grace:
Believe in blessings beyond measure

"Now, faith is the substance of things hoped for, the evidence of things not seen."
Hebrews 11:1

I love the "Faith Chapter" of the Bible, (Hebrews 11:1). Faith and hope are equivalent. Faith requires a <u>vision</u> of hope. Abel, Enoch, Noah, Abraham, Esau, Jacob, Joseph, Rahab, Gideon, Barak, Samson and David are spoken of in the "Faith Chapter" and should be examples to us of what faith can accomplish. Verse 33 says that *"Kingdoms were subdued"* and then continuing on to the end of the chapter, Paul describes how faith paid off for all of the people. A man without faith cannot please God (Verse 6). I have faith and a vision of hope for a complete recovery and healing from cancer.

I believe God has a purpose for my healing. I am convinced there is eternal hope and that it is mine! I should have a vision, a dream, a purpose, a goal for my life. Without one of these I am as a wandering man, void of hope! Knowing God and having Jesus as my Savior is my provision of faith and hope. I Cor. 15:19 says, *"If in this life only you have hope in Christ, you are of all men most miserable"*. I have faith in God, hope for an eternity in heaven and blessings beyond measure In between! Those blessings (beyond measure and in between) will include my complete and total healing.

"Dancing With God"

Daily Dose of Grace:
"Stay in step, let God lead."

"I will guide thee with my eyes, instruct thee and teach thee."
Psalm 32:8

We have a beautiful little granddaughter who loves her Papa and Grammy. She also loves to dance! We "crank up" the music; on good days, I lift her in my arms and sway with her or we dance free style. Her Papa lets her stand on top of his feet and as he moves about the room so does she, gliding in rhythm with the music. She loves it! He guides her safely as they dance. His eyes are constantly on her so she doesn't fall. (Psalms 32:8) One step at a time they dance!

I love how the word "guidance" can be easily used as an acronym. G – God, U – You, I – I, DANCE! It gives me a whole new perspective of God my Guide! I know as long as I hold on to God, follow at His rhythm and trust Him, we can dance successfully!! The Psalmist David says so in Psalm 32:8. As long as I obey the Leader, the dance through life will be smooth and precise. My dance through chemo-therapy will be successful! I will try my hardest to stay in the rhythm of the dance (plan) and hang on as God leads. This life dance with Him is SO promising!

"Grace to the Least"

Daily Dose of Grace:
God's Grace is on purpose

"But by the grace of God I am what I am: and his grace which was bestowed upon me was not in vain;........"
I Corinthians 15:10

The Apostle Paul is one of my favorite writers. I think because he is so common-place, so down-to-earth, so honest and proliferate! He considered himself the "least" of the Apostles and "not worthy" to be called an Apostle. He knew his past and where God had brought him from and declared, *"By the grace of God, I am what I am".* God's unmerited favor brought Paul from a murderer to a servant. He even said it was because of God's grace he was able to labor so productively. He said, *"Yet not I, but the GRACE of God, which was with me".* Paul never gave credit to himself for his success as an Apostle.

I know that by God's grace I am what I am! I could never earn or be worthy of God's grace! I'm not great but I have a great notion to serve a great God <u>with all my being</u>. By His grace and through His greatness He saved me and by the same means He will heal me! He feeds me daily, like a bird feeding from bread crumbs on the window seal; I will feed on His inspiration, His daily doses of healing and direction in my life. I praise Him for His grace! **My God is Graceful!**

"A Walk of Integrity"

Daily Dose of Grace:
An honorable spirit is of great worth

"Counsel in the heart of man is like deep water; but a man of understanding will draw it out. A just man walketh in his integrity: his children are blessed after him."
Proverbs 20:5, 7

Proverbs chapter 20 is packed with integrity advice for me today! Integrity is defined as "of worth", "of value", "honorable" and "of goodness"! What wisdom Solomon had!! I will guard the integrity of my heart and ask God for direction.

We have all been given great pieces of wisdom from the Word, but are we going to take it to heart? Prov. 20:5 says, *"Counsel in the heart of a man is like deep water but who will draw it out?"* We must reach down into the depths of God's Word (His wisdom and guidance) and glean from it! In Prov.20:6, Solomon says men like to brag of their own goodness, but can their faithfulness be found? Verse 27 says, *"The spirit of man is the candle of the Lord, searching all the inner parts of the belly"*. There is no hiding from God, the true spirit of our hearts.

I'm dealing with a spirit of the heart today. I want to know from whence it comes. Physically I don't have a lot of energy (strength) to expel, but my mind still works and I have had much time to ponder, where I've been, what I have done and where I am going. God has been my ALL in ALL! I want to be sure that I walk in integrity and that God is the Author of the spirit of my heart, the spirit to resign from my church staff position. I've been on leave since the first of January and it is May already. I don't see a "soon" return and have such a love for Children's Ministry and know I can't work it from a distance; at the same time it must not suffer from neglect. God is my Judge; it is Him I seek, not the will of man. God is my Redeemer, my Friend. He has made the hearing ear, the seeing eye (Verse 12) and I lean on Him for perfect peace.

"I praise You, Father for opportunities to serve you over the years. You've grown me up to love to serve (twenty-five plus years as a church volunteer and fourteen years as a "minister" to children and youth). I count on Your intercession and divine guidance as to "how" I serve in the years ahead! All glory and honor I give to You! Open my ears that I might hear and my eyes that I might see. May my walk be one of integrity!

"Of a Ready Mind"

Daily Dose of Grace:
Humility will bring exaltation

"Humble yourselves therefore under the mighty hand of God, that he may exalt you in due time; Casting all your care upon him; for he careth for you."
I Peter 5:5-6

Peter, an Apostle, gave some worthy advice to Christians throughout areas he traveled. He knew they needed encouragement; he reminded them of the importance of Christ being the cornerstone of their lives. His afflictions encouraged them to walk in Godliness, to love one another, to be strong; and to always to pull from their faith and to continue to serve! **(I Peter 4:16, 19; I Peter 5:2-3, 5-7, 10)**

Nowhere in God's Word have I ever read that <u>life</u> would be a "bed of roses". Many times, we Christians have a tendency to "expect the ROSEY road", just because we are "saved". Saved does not make us exempt from the trials and afflictions of the devil, it gives us great comfort in knowing that our God will walk beside us through those challenges in life.

I am of *"of a ready mind"* (5:2) and I will not be ashamed to give God the praise in my suffering (4:16). I am humbled before Him, under his hand, His mighty hand, believing for everything there is a purpose and as Peter says in 5:2, *"In due time you will be exalted"*. I must be strong (steadfast) in the faith, not give up and remember as Peter says in 5:10 that the God of Grace (undeserved favor) who has given us the promise of eternal glory in His Son, Jesus, will make us perfect, <u>settle</u> and <u>strengthen</u> us after we've suffered a while. I'm so glad I know the God that cares! He longs for me to give all my cares to Him, (5:7).

God wants me to remember, I am His and He is mine through every challenge life may bring my way – *"His mind is stayed on me" and* I will remain of *"a ready mind"*.

Thank you Father for constant reminders of your presence. Your Word speaks hope and healing and I believe!!

"Satan Laughs When I Cry"

Daily Dose of Grace:
Defying Satan will cause him to run

"Submit yourselves therefore to God. Resist the devil, and he will flee. Humble yourselves in the sight of the Lord, and he shall lift you up."
James 4:7, 10

There have been some recent days when I have felt so weak and sick that I have cried! I Peter 5:8 says that *"The devil walks about as a roaring lion, seeking whom he may devour"*. I know he must <u>laugh</u> when I cry! He thinks he is winning but I have news for him! Tears he causes will not blur my vision of a most Holy God!!

I love the story of Lazarus' resurrection in John 11:33-44. Jesus had such compassion for His best friend, Lazarus. His compassion went to Lazarus' sisters, He WEPT. He was compelled to prove to the crowd, when there is hope and faith, there is victory. Lazarus rose from the dead and many came to believe after seeing the miracle.

When I cry, I am crying to God for continued faith and strength and He is right beside me. Victory is Jesus, *"For the Son of man is come, NOT to destroy men's lives, but to save them."* (Luke 9:56) I delight in the promise (Rev 20:10) that in the end Satan will be bound, thrown into the bottomless pit and burn <u>forever</u>: His time on earth is <u>now</u>, but he won't win with me!! I submit myself, my body, my healing to God. I will *"resist the devil"* and *"humble myself in the sight of the Lord,* and the last laugh will be on Satan because *"He (God) will lift me up.* (James 4:7, 10)

Father, thank you for your compassion, for wiping my tears and lifting me up! I'm Yours!!

"A Sailboat with No Wind"

Daily Dose of Grace:
God provides the "good" wind that will keep you on course

"Hast thou not known? Hast thou not heard, that the everlasting God, the Lord, the Creator of the ends of the earth, fainteth not, neither is weary? There is no searching of his understanding. He giveth power to the faint; and to them that have no might he increaseth strength.
Isaiah 40:28-29

I love to watch a sailboat on the open water. Its movement seems so graceful and free. But, I know that in order for it to sail; the sails MUST be hoisted and the wind must be potent, otherwise it is "dead" in the water, propelled only by the motion of the waves! Today I am tired. My physical energy is zapped. I feel like a sailboat dead in the water.

About 10 days ago, my physical body was sailing smoothly and my strength was gaining, then the "wind" was suddenly clipped from my sails. Of what use is *"A Sailboat With no Wind"*? If a sailboat has no wind, the Captain probably grabs an oar and starts to paddle or if very fortunate, tosses a tow rope to another vessel. When I lost my strength to stand or to walk, Sam hung on to me (physically), and on days of IV's and injections, strength began to return. Isaiah 40:28 says that God *"the Creator does not faint"* or get tired! My physical and Spiritual strength come from God. **My God is majestic!**

The class-A personality that I have, makes it very important to me to desire to run; I want to be stronger! I want to be the same "fast paced, full speed ahead" woman. Isaiah 40:31 says, *"They that wait upon the Lord shall renew their strength'.*

God's message to me today is, *"Slow down and wait".* In all of His majesty He has revealed to me, that if I remain obedient and patient in my healing, I'll have *"the strength of eagles wings",* I will *"Run and not be weary, I will walk and not faint!* **I am a sailboat, maneuvering rough waters. God is my Captain and my Wind!**

"Abiding in God's Call"

Daily Dose of Grace:
Catch a dream, rest, recuperate and re-focus

"For he that is called in the Lord, being a servant is the Lord's freeman: likewise also he that is called, being free, is Christ's servant. Ye are bought with a price; be not ye the servants of men."
I Corinthians 7:22-23

Over these months of treatment and restoration, God has not allowed me to forget my "calling". I am still His servant! My mind still works and though I can't physically endure the daily work routine, He has my mind constantly working and contemplating obedience to His call. I will keep my mind busy, dream dreams and pursue direction.

Through my "writing" (3 books of my dreams) and my enduring love for children and youth ministry, I know God will continue to use me. I sit some nights with little sleep because of things (possibilities) in my mind and I continue to call on God for direction. I want to be "where" He wants me and do "what" pleases Him"! I long for assurance that these dreams (thoughts) are what He has given me! I am *called of the Lord, a servant, the Lord's freeman: I am bought with a price……….."* (I Cor. 7:22-23).

God isn't finished with me yet! I'm "FREE" to dreams and pursuit, and long for HIS direction in all I do! **My God is glorious!** I believe He has given me this time to REST, RECUPERATE, and RE-DIRECT. By His glory and grace I'll be UP and GOING soon and He'll have me UP and DOING

His work! I praise Him for wisdom and direction in the days, weeks, months and years to come! He's healing me for a lifetime of obedience to His call! Could my dreams be contagious? I hope so! Would you catch a dream with me?

"Standing the Test, Saying Thank You"

Daily Dose of Grace:
Healing is a work in progress

"I have fought a good fight, I have finished my course, I have kept the faith."
II Timothy 4:8

Some days it is really hard to get over the miserable feelings of sickness. Some days I ask myself "Why"! Why did I choose the route of chemo-therapy! Constantly, though, I am reminded by my doctor and family members that, though discomfort is <u>now</u>, long-term benefits will <u>outweigh</u> the discomfort (suffering). I won't allow miserable feelings to outweigh my hope!

To be able to laugh at my bald head, my caps and scarves and the quiet (sometimes verbal) observations of my grandchildren is uplifting. I was fearful that my appearance would frighten them. I've found that my own "gloom" is silly. I must envision myself as a "work of healing" in progress! I must *"finish the course and fight the good fight"* (II Timothy 4:2-8.

I KNOW that my hair will return and I will cherish it as a "crown" of life! (James 1:12) I will have endured the trials of sickness, yet I will have held on to my faith in the Healing God and the promise that NEW LIFE would come. A growth of new hair will be my crown of righteousness.

Thank You Father for new hope! May I always be able to boast, and say as Paul, "I've fought the good fight, I've finished the course, and I've kept the faith." II Timothy 4:7

"Heart Love"

Daily Dose of Grace:
God is a discerning and loving Liberator

"Beloved, if God so loved us, we ought also to love one another."
I John 4:11

Yesterday was such a special day! An uplifting came my way when a kind and caring couple (Mike and Joann) from my church stopped by to deliver a hand full of home-made get well cards from the 3rd grade AWANA class. Earlier in the day I had received a card in the mail, from a 2nd grader! These were cards that said, "I love you, God loves you, get well, I miss you". Along with the cards came pictures of each author, so I felt such a special connection. Heart love is a welcome alliance!

I was encouraged to hear that EVERY week in AWANA; the Kids say a prayer for me. Oh the caring little hearts of children! I am so thankful that in their innocence and sincerity, they love from deep within their tender hearts! We, as adults, can learn a lesson from the children. We are an apathetic people! We have become so busy we don't take time to perform an act of kindness, to remember or even to pick up the phone! We are lethargic in HEART LOVE!

God brings me back to my own failed promises and words like "I love you, I'll pray for you or I'll call you". Empty words (promises) are unrewarding! I know, and pray I will discern appropriately and love from the heart!!

God gave me Psalm 31, as I pondered, disappointedly, some disconnections over the past weeks. David said, *"I rejoice in your mercies, you know my trouble, you know my soul is in trouble"*. David said that even his neighbors and acquaintances turned from him. He felt like *"a dead man, a broken vessel"*. (Psalm 31: 7, 11, 12).

I believe HEART LOVE produces faithful prayers, connections, and encouragement and that heart love will liberate *"the dead man and the broken vessel"*. I'm so thankful that God and little children love from the heart. *"I trust in Him, He is my God"*. (Psalm 31:14).

Love is a heart thing! I long for heart love as the children have given! We should cultivate a culture of "NOT too busy to love", cast our disappointments and disconnections to the wind and believe God can change hearts. I John 3:18 admonishes us to *"Not love in words or by our tongue, but by deeds and truth"*. I commit to cast out "busy-ness" from my life, share love more and someday to reap the rewards God has for me (the doer). There are people everywhere who have love needs in trying times!

Thank you Father, for courage and strength. My hope is in You! Help people everywhere to grow to understand real love. Today is going to be a good day!.

"Going Through for Others"

Daily Dose of Grace:
God comforts me so I can comfort others

"Blessed be………..the Father of mercies and the God of all comfort."
I Corinthians 1:3

As I maneuvered slowly and cautiously about the house this morning, pushing for strength, struggling to make the bed without needing to sit down and rest before I finished; thoughts infiltrated my mind.   Thoughts of self-encouragement, *"Come on you can do this!"* You see, I am a person who does not believe that constant "sitting" will give me strength. I believe I MUST have the <u>spirit</u> and the <u>will</u> to "push" toward the goal! I depend totally on God for strength in reaching the goal and He gives me added strength to push, but He also sits me down to rest! **My God is merciful!**

I must follow His guidance in this "healing process".   In John 16:33, Jesus said, *"In the world you will have <u>tribulation</u>, but be of good cheer, I have over come the world".* Just as Jesus Christ will put the world under His feet; He will help me to put cancer under my feet!! Perhaps my "going through" will be a lesson learned so I can help others "go through".   There's a purpose in this journey.

I pray to God, no one I love, will ever have to experience the affects of chemo-therapy. Because I have "suffered", I don't want others to. Sympathy (what I could feel in the past) will, in the future, be empathy, because I've been there.   II

Corinthians 1:4 spells out the purpose of tribulation, *"That we may be able to comfort them who are in trouble; by the comfort we ourselves were comforted."*

If "Going Through for Others" is God's purpose for me, I'm on it! How can He use me to comfort others? I wait for His direction.

"Sufficient Grace"

Daily Dose of Grace:
God's surrounding grace is all I need

"......., My grace is sufficient for thee: for my strength is made perfect in weakness......"
II Corinthians 12:9

Some days of this journey are good, some days are bad. Like the Apostle Paul, with the thorn in his flesh (his physical condition) I Cor. 12:7-9, these cancer treatments have become "thorns" in my flesh. I am overcome with joy and thankfulness that God's grace is sufficient for me (II Cor. 12:9). God has reminded me that His grace connection outweighs friendship connections.

God gets me thru the hurt and disappointment. He reminds me to love and of HIS every day omnipresence and "sufficient grace". He says, *"I am with you, that is ALL you need!"* (II Cor. 12:9). I am always "surrounded" by His grace. Paul said he was happy about the thorn in his flesh. He said, in essence, *"The less I have, the more I depend on God".* (II Cor. 12:10)

Thank You, Father, that you can always be depended upon. You'll never leave me or forsake me! Thank You for the GRACE connection and for being my Always Personable God!

"Suffering but Not Forgotten"

Daily Dose of Grace:
God wants you to be an active example of faith

"That the trial of your faith, being much more precious than of gold that perisheth, though it be tried with fire, might be found unto praise and honour and glory at the appearing of Jesus Christ:"
I Peter 1:6-7

Suffering comes in various forms; physically, emotionally, and spiritually. It is a universal occurrence; none of us humans are exempt! It was never God's desire that mankind suffer but when Adam and Eve chose knowledge of good and evil by eating of the forbidden fruit, they brought about the beginning of suffering; something that had not been known before but we will, (until we get to heaven), have to deal with.

I thank God that someday we won't have to deal with pain and hurt anymore, our bodies will be made perfect. I don't believe God takes any <u>honor</u> in my physical suffering. Pain and disease do not come from Him; they are the evil attacks of Satan who takes joy in causing me much pain, sickness and discomfort.

God is my Refuge and my Strength, my **<u>very present help</u>** in these times. He will not leave me comfortless! **My God is Impartial!** I'm turning my faith on and I am trying! Just this morning, I was trying to find strength to <u>just make the bed</u> and found myself weeping and crying out to God, *"God, just give me some strength to finish this task, to make it through the day and in to tomorrow!"* Sam came into the room and said,

"Honey, just don't do this, come on back to your chair, God put me here to help you!"   My reply was, "I MUST push, and I MUST try!" I really believe God expects me to put forth an effort to grow stronger!!   I like to use the light bulb as an example – God gave us the wisdom of that great invention and electricity, but we have to turn on the switch to receive the benefit! WISHING for light won't bring it! SO! I believe just "WISHING" for strength won't bring it!

God wants me to turn my "faith" on and "try"! I'm thankful He hasn't forgotten me and I believe He takes glory in an <u>active example of faith</u>!

"Emotionally Drained"

Daily Dose of Grace:
God helps me through emotional moments

"The righteous cry and the Lord hears, and delivers them out of all their troubles. The Lord is near to the brokenhearted, and saves those who are crushed in the spirit."
Psalm 34:17-18

I try to keep a positive attitude but I have to be honest, when I feel so weak, physically, my emotions get the best of me. I try really hard NOT to cry in the presence of my family because I want their spirits to remain high. I prefer they see "strength" in me.

Writing about my feelings is a great comfort. It helps me to face my weakness and also to understand that it's O.K. to have those moments; it's part of the healing process. Elijah (I Kings 19), Moses (Numbers 11), and David (all through Psalms) had their emotional moments.

No person should condemn or point a finger at a person who is emotionally torn. It does not mean they are weak or morally deserving! Emotional pain is very real in the healing process and it makes me see God more as merciful and full of compassion. My "emotional breaks" help me draw closer to Him!

Scripture like Psalm 34:17-18, helps me deal with those troubles! GOD ousts my "Emotionally Drained" mood and PICKS ME UP to **new hope!!** I am ever grateful for his perpetually available Word that upholds me in those emotional moments.

"Gold in the Kingdom"

Daily Dose of Grace:
Healing is a refining process

"And he shall sit as a refiner and purifier of silver: and he shall purify the sons of Levi, and purge them as gold and silver, that they may offer unto the Lord an offering in righteousness."
Malachi 3:3

God gave me a song today! I love good Christian contemporary and gospel music because the messages speak to the heart. One of the side affects of cancer rehabilitation is "depression". Music helps me forget to be depressed and lifts my spirit!

God's Word gives me hope in the purging and refining process of healing. The Prophet Malachi had been sent to proclaim the message of the coming of John the Baptist who would come to call to repentance, to refine, purify and make righteous, a wicked nation! God has put songwriters among us who can pen and present His Word, hope and promises in the form of music that can help in the healing process.

The inability to move quickly, do lots of things, get in my car and go somewhere, work in my flower garden and in my house and the search for strength and energy to prevail has been difficult. My impatience is obvious! Depression hits me and the four walls close in on me and then I begin to "almost" want to give up! But God always COMES THROUGH and today He gave me a song and it was as if He was singing it to me! Get this; it was about GOLD! In the song it says when we are thinking, *"When will it end, how can I go on; don't give up, don't give in, look to the light, there's <u>Gold in the Ashes</u>"*. There have been days when I have wanted to give up or give in but God always shows me the gold is possible even in the fire!

Fire is refining and it is a process of producing precious and shining gold. I believe that to mean, I'll be coming back stronger and better than ever! Chemo-therapy is a fire, a process to produce healing. Cancer will become ashes and under those ashes will be a stronger woman than ever before, a better servant (Gold in the Kingdom).

God continues to have a work for me to do and I wait on His discernment and direction. I desire that He put me where I can shine the MOST <u>for Him</u>. Paraphrasing I Peter 1:7, *"Trials are a test of faith, testing strength and purity. My faith is more precious to God than gold and as gold stands the test of fire,* so will I in this journey and be as pure as gold. I LONG TO SHINE ON AND BE "Gold in the Kingdom"!

"Courage Equals Patience"

Daily Dose of Grace:
Be courageous when in pain and wise enough to wait

"Wait on the Lord; be of good courage, and He will strengthen your heart; wait I say, on the Lord."
Psalm 27:14

In all the years of my life I have never "needed" the courage that I have needed over the past 3 months. Courage was needed in the very beginning, after diagnosis. It was necessary for "choices" we had to make. I say "we" because my husband has been my great encourager and he has been a part of the choices we've made! Choosing is ONE thing, but FOLLOWING THROUGH is another.

First, was the wisdom and courage to choose the path of treatment and rehab? The BIGGIES have been the courage to accept the side-affects and the patience to persevere. The hope for victory at the end of the battle encourages my perseverance.

My doctors, nurses, family and friends are my encouragers. Just as Joshua encouraged his army in Joshua 10:25, *"Don't be afraid, don't be dismayed (discouraged), be strong and of good courage, the Lord will (secure) all your enemies against whom you fight".* I know Satan is the enemy, the one who would love to see me lose the battle. (He's the one who has brought it to me), but his will shall be defeated!

Patience has been the biggest challenge for me. God's Word gives me courage and wisdom to be patient. David speaks it most clearly in Psalms 27:14, when he says, *"Wait on the Lord"*. I know my strength will come if I will just be patient! My prayer today is, "God give me <u>courage</u> to be <u>patient</u>". Courage is not the absence of fear but the ability to face it!

"God, give me the ability to be patient in the healing process".

"Hanging on to Hope!"

Daily Dose of Grace:
I can bring a morsel of hope to a friend

"We are afflicted in every way, but not crushed; perplexed, but not despairing; persecuted, but not forsaken; struck down but not destroyed."
II Corinthians 4:8-9

I have a wonderful neighbor who is going through cancer treatments. We were both diagnosed within days apart. His cancer is different and more severe; his treatments more extensive. We spend time encouraging each other, greeting over the fence, counting down the days until treatments are completed. We visit and talk about the challenges! We've had such beautiful weather over the past weeks we can sit outside and enjoy nature as we visit. So much of our experiences are the same, we can look at each other and say, "Been there, done that". I like to tease him by saying, *"What's up with you still having all that hair and I'm BALD!! Something's not right with this deal!"*

We also talk about how blessed we are to have wonderful spouses who are giving so much of themselves to encourage and help us in recovery. One day last week as we were conversing, I remember saying to him several times, *"We're gonna make it, this will all come to pass, we'll be stronger than ever before!"* He was having a really painful day! I wanted to encourage him to HANG ON TO HOPE, because in his pain I could see him wanting to "die", to give up. His wife dispenses his medication to ease the pain. He doesn't like medicine but eventually gives in to take it! I have felt what he feels; <u>not so much pain</u>, but we have a comradeship because we fight the same battle! I want him to see HOPE in me and grasp the REAL HOPE, in CHRIST.

My new challenge in these days is to *"Sanctify Christ as Lord in my heart, always be ready to make a defense to Him, if He asks and to give account for the HOPE that is in me, but with gentleness and reverence"*. (I Peter 3:15). My neighbor's wife is a faithful believer and prayer warrior! Perhaps together we can encourage "Fly" to cast all his cares on God! I want him to know and believe there is REAL HOPE, everlasting and eternal. I have "reached for" and am "Hanging on to Hope".

"So Good, So God"

Daily Dose of Grace:
God knows my needs before I ask

"And we know that all things work together for good to them that love God, to them who are the called according to his purpose."
Romans 8:28

Just last week I received in the mail a music CD from a caring, loving and faithful couple who are dear friends to us (Terry & Linda). I've played it over and over because there is so much encouragement, promises and hope in each song. It has really lifted my spirits, reminded me of God's goodness and nourished my faith. I listen to it and feel God "hugging" me!

Sometimes when we go through hard times we can easily fall into our own "pity party"; whether it is sickness, conflict, disappointment, financial crisis, or stress. (The list could go on!) I have this great promise that God always knows my needs, even before I ask, Romans 8:26-27. I need God hugs on most days!

So many times I have to pinch myself and snap out of pity and remember "all things" (even sickness) can work for my good because of "WHO" my Father is! I am believing I will come back healthier, stronger and yes, even **beautiful** because God is in control and He is working on me!

Today I have Mother's old Bible on my lap. She was an avid Bible reader and has great Scriptures marked. Today's passage, she marked with a reference to Phil. 4:6-7 which paraphrased says, *"Don't worry about anything, rather pray about everything, tell God what you need and don't forget to say thank You He answers, If you do this, you will have peace".*

I have His peace and I know "all things work together for good". I think it'll be SO GOOD in the days to come I won't be able to stand it!! I'll be saying *"Look at me, see how FAST I move, see how STRONG I am, see my NEW and BETTER hair"!* Now step back and watch me on my journey to 102 years of age! Scriptures like these today, remind me to laugh, and say *"It's SO GOOD, SO GOD!"* **Peace, hope and promise equal much laughter! My God is Good!**

"Life's Crossroads"

Daily Dose of Grace:
"Wait and look to God for direction"

"Ponder the path of thy feet and let all thy ways be established."
Proverbs 4:26

It is hard to imagine that there is quickly approaching another <u>crossroads</u> in my life. Truth is, we really think about all those crossroads (choices) coming when we're younger, but I'm finding there are crossroads, even now.

The wisdom of Solomon reminds me of the "seriousness" of choices at the crossroads: *"Enter not into the path of the wicked, and go not in the way of the evil man, avoid it, turn from it and pass away."* Proverbs 4: 14-15. I must "always" *<u>"Ponder the path of my feet"</u>* Proverbs 4:26.

I have to say, in my younger days I didn't <u>always</u> seek God's way! I remember many sermons and Sunday School lessons on Matthew 7:13-14. I knew that Jesus said *"Enter into the straight gate, and the narrow way that leads to life, few will find it."* But! When you're "sowing wild oats", "dreaming man-made dreams" and "reaching for the stars", sometimes you forget to <u>look to God,</u> to wait on His direction!

Today, I wait and look to God's direction at the crossroads of full-time ministry and concentration on healing, recovery and writing. God has made it clear to me that money is not the objective. I don't NEED to work; I do need to mend physically!

Thinking back, 41 years is a long time to work! I've always given to every position I have ever held, whether as a waitress, a clerk, an administrator or as a minister to children and youth, my EVERY BIT of energy and attention. The crossroads tells me perhaps "family", "healing" and "listening" is the direction I should go! The past 3 ½ months has allowed me much time to contemplate my destination and reflect my past.

I must put my full attention on God; listen, pray and watch for signs along the way! I know that in His perfection, He has a plan for me because **my God is perfect!**

Father, I thank You in advance for the process and completion of healing. At this crossroads, please hold my hand, kick back any stones that may hinder my passage, break any barriers to obedience and lead the way! Your choice will be mine and I will be blessed at this "Crossroads of my Life".

"Reason to Survive"

Daily Dose of Grace:
God gives strength for the journey and a reason to survive

"……….and now, lo, I am this day fourscore and five years old. As yet I am as strong this day as I was in the day that Moses sent me, as my strength was then, even so is my strength now, for war, but to go out and to come in. Now, give me this mountain……"
Joshua 14:10-12

This past week has been the toughest of all for me. I've been thinking, WOA…….I didn't just get hit by a big truck, this time, **it ran over me!** I need STAMINA to survive!

The medical professionals tell me it's the "cumulative" affect; the number of treatments adds to the discomfort. Hmmmmm….! They didn't tell me about that before! When I think back, yes, each treatment added a few extra days to my recovery time. There is still "Much to Conquer". Just as God told Joshua, *"There remaineth yet very much land to be possessed"* (Joshua 13:1), He has reminded me there is REASON to survive!

Today my daughter, Holly, and granddaughter, Keira visited and brought me a beautiful pot of flowers and a card! On the card, Holly wrote: "For the #1 survivor. Mom, we love you the most!" Keira ran with open arms to greet me and was just so pleased to present me with the flowers!

These are the sorts of moments that add STAMINA to my journey. The flowers are transplantable and I will add them to my front garden in a few days, then each year I'll delight in their beauty and remember <u>I HAVE SURVIVED</u>! God will keep me alive for a reason, and *"as my strength was, so it shall be"*. With God we conquer much!

"Conquering with Courage, Hope and Heart"

Daily Dose of Grace:
You can be courageous and strong when You have faith

"Nay, in all these things we are more than conquerors through him that loved us."
Romans 9:35

I am a conqueror! To conquer means to achieve, to win, and to face a challenge with high hopes and strength of heart. Our oldest daughter refers to me as "invincible". I prefer the title warrior, conqueror and courageous. God's love is "invincible"! No matter what trials or persecutions we must face in life, they cannot separate us from God's love.

God's Word gives me HOPE! Previous tribulations (mountains and valleys of life), have given me "courage" to pursue. I believe that past experiences and conquests play an important role in current battles we face. The conquest of old battles stirs my courage and reminds me to hope. In my heart I believe God and I will be the "victors" in this cancer battle!

Joshua said in Joshua 10:25, *"Fear not nor be dismayed, be Strong and of good courage"*. He goes on to say, God will deal with the enemies that we fight. God is my LIFELINE! **My God is invincible**! My HOPE is in HIM!

My neighbor, "Fly", has lung cancer. He was diagnosed about the same time as I was. I have tried to be his cheerleader and have encouraged him to look up and not give up! His recovery will be a harder battle than mine because his ENEMY (kind of cancer) is more destructive.

"Fly" has always been a healthy man, he has not had to battle for his life before and he does not have that hope and courage to conquer! He lacks the "armor" of experience because he has not had to fight before. He needs to be reminded of the "armor" of faith! That armor will give him courage, hope and the heart to conquer!

Today I will visit "Fly" in the hospital (he's been there 2 weeks). I dread the trip, but feel compelled to be his cheerleader, to encourage him. I pray that when I leave his room, he'll know I'm cheering for him and that his heart will be renewed (stirred) with strength. Satan would love to see him leave this world, weak and without hope. I pray my visit will show him MORE of God and give him strength and hope for the journey. *"Come on Fly, you, I and God can do this!"*

"God Walks the Dark Hills"

Daily Dose of Grace:
God's presence brings light and peace in days of darkness

"But ye are a chosen generation, a royal priesthood, an holy nation, a peculiar people; that ye should shew forth the praises of him who hath called you out of darkness into his marvelous light."
I Peter 2:9

The old southern gospel song that talks about the "dark hills of life" and reminds us that God walks them with us. I love that old song; it gives me peace. As God's children we never have to walk the dark hills alone. There are days when I feel alone and I need this reminder!

Psalm 112:4, tells me that *"To the upright there is LIGHT in the darkness"*. That Light is the Father. The verse goes on to say that *"God is gracious, compassionate and righteous"*. I'm so glad for the Light, without Him, days would be darker. When I am lying in the darkness at night, feeling weak, feeling really bad, wanting to give up, He's within a HUG away! So many times I've cried out for a hug; He's never let me down!

"Through the tender mercy of our God, the Dayspring from on high has visited ME to give light to ME who sits in darkness and in the shadow of death, to guide MY feet in the way of peace". (Luke 1:78-79) Oh the peace that His presence brings!! I will let it be known to all that God is the "Light" through the dark hills of my journey. **My God is Compassionate!** I Peter 2:9 tells me I am *"chosen"*, *"holy"*, *"peculiar"* and *"royal"* and that I should

"praise Him who has called me out of darkness into His marvelous light".

I will never cease to praise Him for His presence and guidance in my life. I will always look to the Light in my days of darkness. When He is ready to call me home, I will gladly take my flight into eternal light (heaven). I believe in the deepest of my soul that I am being healed to completion, for a season! He still has things for me to do on earth!

If I ascend up into heaven, thou art there: if I make my bed in hell, behold, thou art there. If I take wings of the morning, and dwell in the uttermost parts of the sea; Even there shall thy hand lead me, and thy right hand shall hold me.
Psalm 139:8-10

"Setting Sail for Home"

Daily Dose of Grace:
Following God's plan will bring you home

"But thou, O Lord, art a God full of compassion, and gracious, longsuffering, and plenteous in mercy and truth."
Psalm 86:15

You have heard the statement, *"There is light at the end of the tunnel"*. We all know that the closer we get to OUT, the brighter the light becomes.

In the beginning weeks of chemotherapy I remember writing about *"The Map for My Journey"*. A first time journey can be perhaps frightening, challenging, exciting and rewarding. I think of the journeys of the Apostle Paul; the 40 year journey of the Israelites (in a circle), Joseph's journey to fame and Jesus' journey to the cross, just to name a few. So life IS a JOURNEY!

When Jesus called out the Disciples, He told them not to bring their coats, or money, but just to follow His leading. There was no map; the journey would be one of FAITH! I love Jeremiah 1:5, God's words to Jeremiah, *"Before I formed you, I knew you"*! God's plan for me was before my conception. He knew this cancer journey was coming and He knew He would be the wind beneath my wings!

Yesterday I began phase two of chemotherapy. The change of drugs weren't as potent! I came home "feeling good"! Imagine that!! The Doctor told me the change would spare me MUCH discomfort and I would GET UP much more quickly!! Yesterday was a memorable day, a great landmark! I will also get a 2 week break!! I see the Light!!

I praise God for being a *"compassionate God, a gracious God, a longsuffering God, and a merciful and truthful God"*. (Psalm 86:15). Today I'm *Setting Sail for Home*. Who could ask for a better Travel Companion? He was there when I drew the first breath of life and He runs with me today! Thanks to prayer warriors who have cheered me along the way!

Celebrate with me! God has given me a SECOND WIND!!

"Love Won't Let Go"

Daily Dose of Grace:
Real love is measured by the flight of feet, not by the flapping of the tongue

"Beloved, let us love one another: for love is of God; and everyone that loveth is born of God, and knoweth God. He that loveth not knoweth not God; for God is love."
I John 4:7-8

"He brought me to His banqueting table; His banner over me is love". I do so remember that little song, "His Banner over Me is Love". We have sung it over all these years with the children. Over the past weeks and months that song has brought a whole new perspective to my life. Although there have been days of depression, sickness and at times wanting to give up, I've thrilled at the "closeness" of my Father! His *Love Won't Let Go*.

While close to my chair on many a day, I have banqueted with my Father. He wraps His arms around me, holds me close and assures me that I am surrounded, draped, covered with a banner of love! I have banqueted on His Word and scrambled for passages when He'd say to me things like, *"My Love Wont' Let Go"*, *"I Walk the Dark Hills"*, *"My Grace is Sufficient"*, *"You've Suffered but you are not Forgotten"*. God's love is beyond my comprehension!

If there is ONE thing I'd desire for all men to know, it is that God commands us to love! I John 4:7-8 and John 15:11. Paul wrote in the Epistle to the Hebrews, *"Let brotherly love*

93

continue" and *"Remember them that are in bonds <u>as bound with them</u>"*. (Hebrews 13:1, 3) He also said in Romans 13:8 *"Owe no man anything <u>but to love one another</u>"*.

KUDOS to Andrea and Janea who have been ladies of excellence, role models of exhibited love. They've called, stopped by, sent cards and shared inspiration regularly in so many ways! They have done this because they are "bound" with me; we are bonded in "love" and friends love at all times.

I have been reminded of my own failure to put feet to love. We should never be so busy as to not love! Proverbs 17:17 says, *"A friend loveth at all times"*. It is time to put action to words, *"Love not only in word, but in deed"*. **INDEED!**

Thank you Father for this valuable lesson. Continue to remind me, REAL <u>Love Won't Let Go</u>. Thanks for being a Loving God!

"Perseverance and Prayer"

Daily Dose of Grace:
Always believe in the power of prayer

"Pray, ask in the spirit, watch with perseverance (diligently) for all saints. Happy are those who endure, as Job; the Lord is of tender mercy".
Ephesians 6:18, James 5:11

Yesterday, God placed a complete stranger in my path who said to me, *"Prayer accomplishes so much, I will pray for you".* I was so moved! This man had never seen me, but knew by my appearance that I was undergoing chemo treatments. He was a man of compassion and said to me, *"Believe in the power of the prayers of the people".* I replied, *"Oh yes! I am healed!"* He said, *"I will pray for your return to perfect health".* I thanked him for caring. I believe in the power of collective prayer. *"The effectual fervent prayer of a righteous man availeth much."* (James 5:16)

Yesterday God sent at least 4 people my way (complete strangers) who had compassion! What a renewed reality – There is POWER in the PRAYERS and PERSEVERANCE of people! I claim total healing and lift up prayers to the One and Only who heals and provides faith and courage to endure!!

"Beyond Imagination"

Daily Dose of Grace:
Imagine and dream for the best in your journey

"Nevertheless I am continually with thee: thou hast holden me by my right hand. Thou shalt guide me with thy counsel, and afterward receive me to glory. Whom have I in heaven but thee? And there is none upon earth that I desire beside thee."
Psalm 73:23-35

Sam and I have had this special privilege to enjoy some "down time" in the Sunshine State the past week. Rest has been wonderful! The wonder of seeing Disney World is <u>Beyond Imagination</u>.

As human beings, we can only "dream" (imagine) what something must be like, before we actually get to experience or see it. Some things we don't care to "imagine"; for instance, the experience of cancer, disease, sickness or pain. We avoid thoughts of those things, we only dream of the **good**!! Whether we "dream" or "avoid", we still don't REALLY know, until we've been there!!

We watch TV commercials, billboards and vacation magazines about the ultimate vacation experiences. Yet only have a picture that expands our imagination! An imagination of what it would be like! We "dream" of the opportunity! Paul says in II Cor. 5:1, *"For we KNOW that if the earthly house of this tabernacle were dissolved, we have a building of God, a house not made with hands, <u>eternal in the heavens</u>.* The promises of

God's Word are our "billboard" (marketing device) of heaven. John got the GRAND TOUR; we have the written Word!

There is a contemporary Christian song that speaks of man's imagination of what heaven will be like. It says, *"I can only imagine......."!* Heaven is incomprehensible. **My God is incomprehensible.** Imagination is our human comprehension of the unknown, of what heaven may be like! Another part of the song says, *"What will my heart feel, when surrounded by God's glory, will I dance with Jesus or will I be stilled by His awe. Will I stand before Him or fall on my knees; will I sing hallelujah or be able to speak at all? I can only imagine!"*

John said, *"I looked and behold, a door was opened in heaven......."* (Rev 4:1) then he proceeds to tell us of his tour. It is difficult for our minds to comprehend what heaven will be like! I'm thankful that as His child, *"I have a home ETERNAL IN THE HEAVENS"* (Psalm 73:23-25), and I will live the reality some day! God is **a God of Promise**!

Before May, 2007 we had not known the reality (experience) of Disney World. Until Feb 2007, I had not known the reality of cancer therapy! "Been there, done that"! All has been "Beyond Imagination". Today I declare; Disney World and cancer have been conquered! One day Heaven will be my home! I can't wait!! I will be speechless as to my knees I will fall!

"Passing the Test of Endurance"

Daily Dose of Grace:
God's goodness endures forever

"Thou therefore, my son, be strong in the grace that is in Christ Jesus. Thou therefore endure hardness, as a good soldier of Jesus Christ."
II Timothy 2:1, 3

While on vacation in Florida, I remember that first day and trusting in a motorized wheel chair (at Sam's insistence) to get me to and fro. Wouldn't you know? About half way through the day; it quit on me. We had to wait for someone to come and bring another chair. After being let down once, I have to tell you, I wasn't very trusting of the 2nd chair.

We spent 14 hours at "Magic Kingdom" that day, yet I determined within myself that another day at a park I would "test my physical endurance" and WALK! I am convinced that every bit of my strength (physical, mental, spiritual), comes from God. My physical strength is returning! All because *"God's goodness endures forever"* (Psalm 136:1); *"The Lord is my strength"* (Psalm 18:2); *"The strength of my life"* (Psalm 27:1) and; *"The strength of my heart"* (Psalm 73:26).

The Apostle Paul encouraged Timothy, *"Thou, therefore endure hardship as a good soldier."* (II Tim. 2:3). I have tried to be a good soldier and have hung on to one of my favorite passages of Scripture, Philippians 4:13, *"I can do all things through Christ, who strengthens me."*

Praise God for renewed strength! On our 2nd day at Disney MGM, I walked! We spend 12 hours there! On our 3rd day we were at Animal Kingdom for 9 hours and I did it!! I have passed the test of endurance and will grow stronger and more determined every day! God <u>HAS NOT</u> AND <u>WILL NEVER</u> let me down! **My God is long-suffering!**

"The Difference Love Makes"

Daily Dose of Grace:
Love will lighten the load of your journey

"Beareth all things, believeth all things, hopeth all things, endureth all things. Charity never faileth:..............."
I Corinthians 13:7-8

In only one month and 8 days Sam and I will celebrate our 40th wedding anniversary! We have traveled many roads together. As I reflect back on all those roads (some rocky, some smooth, some long, some short, some roads of joy, some of sadness), I can only say "LOVE MADE THE DIFFERENCE".

The Apostle Paul gave a most unique and profound definition of love, in I Corinthians chapter 13. This text is a part of so many weddings! Like so many other Bible passages described as "beautiful" and "nice", some people have a tendency to <u>not</u> think of it as prolific! Sometimes we take the word, "love", too lightly.

On Mother's Day our oldest daughter, Kellee, gave me a beautiful bracelet with the words engraved, *"Love endures all, love believes all, love bears all, love hopes all"*, verse 7 of "The Love Chapter"! It made me cry and still does, but my tears are tears of great joy! Joy because God gave me a husband who has "endured all", "believes all", "hopes all" and "bears all"! Right beside me, all the way in these months, he has endured the journey well. He has borne a lot of responsibility (housekeeper, shopper, laundry man, cook and chauffer)! He

101

has believed, with me, in God's healing power and continues to "hope" with me for restoration and a long life!

I KNOW that "Love Makes A Difference"! Never in 40 years have I doubted my husband's love and in these past weeks it's prevalence and the difference it has made is MOST obvious.

God's love makes a difference in our eternal destiny; Sam's love has made a difference in my earthly destiny. It has been a journey of love and worth the living!

"It Will be Alright – Be Happy"

Daily Dose of Grace:
There is peace and happiness in knowing God

"Let not your heart be troubled; ye believe in God, believe also in me."
John 14:1

While on our retreat (vacation), there was a song we heard regularly in the Disney theme parks. It was called, "Okumah Matahta", a really exciting song that was about the overall theme of the year, *"Where Dreams Come True"*. Okumah Matahta means *"It'll be all right, be happy"*. To dream is to hope, to believe. In the Christian aspect we might call it "faith".

Since I was a teenager, one of my most favorite passages in the Bible has been John 14:1-6. How I love that promise! How sad the Disciples must have been, when Jesus told them He was going away! Jesus spent some time comforting and reassuring them. In verse 27, He said, *"Peace I leave with you, my peace I give you…..let not your heart be troubled, neither let it be afraid."* In short, Jesus said, "It'll be all right, be happy", I'll be with you!"

My first thought when I heard the definition of "Okumah Matahta" was of all the well-wishers who have said and still say to me, "It will be alright"! I KNOW it will because of "Who" I know. I will *"Rest in the Lord, and wait patiently on Him"*, (Psalm 37:7).

Solomon, the wisest of all earthly men said, *"Happy is the man that findeth wisdom"*. Wisdom is <u>KNOWING</u> God. Okumah Matahta!

"God Gives a Song"

Daily Dose of Grace:
SING *when God says to*

".......be filled with the spirit; speaking to yourselves in psalms and hymns and spiritual songs, singing and making melody in your heart to the Lord; giving thanks always for all things unto God and the Father in the name of our Lord Jesus Christ."
Ephesians 5:18-20

The Apostle Paul said to the Ephesians that they should <u>sing</u>, <u>make melody</u>, <u>and give thanks</u> through psalms, hymns and songs when filled with the spirit!

I know that words of praise and thanksgiving come forth from my deepest being (spirit) when I least expect it. I may be brushing my teeth, washing dishes, driving down the road or walking in the park when words of praise and thanksgiving come! When God puts a song on my lips, I MUST sing! I cannot hold back when I remember His mercy, grace and love. He gives me the words and the melody!

Today! I ran to retrieve my journal and penned these words: *"I just want to thank You for seeing me through, for holding me close, SO CLOSE to You! I just want to thank You for being my friend, for Your mercy and grace that will never, ever, end. I just want to thank You for loving me so, for all of the ways, You've let me know. Thank You for grace, mercy and love, for so many blessings You've sent from above. I just want to thank You (mercy), I just want to thank You (grace), I just want to thank You (love), thank You (friend). Thank You for being my Friend! "A friend loveth at all times"* (Proverbs 17:17).

Jesus, I call YOU my Friend! Amen.

"Coming Back"

Daily Dose of Grace:
When you want to ask WHY, you should remember God has a Divine Prognosis (outcome) for you

"Then answered the Lord unto Job out of the whirlwind, and said, Gird up thy loins now like a man:"
Job 40: 6-7

I dreaded coming back!! Vacation was SO GOOD! A three week break really spoiled me; I had SO much energy and was "running" again! Now my pace has slowed considerably, and I find myself on Sunday afternoons "dreading" the next day. Today is Monday and here I sit at the Oncology Clinic, just waking up, I'm back!! Every chemo treatment is introduced with a bag of medication for prevention of nausea and vomiting, WONDERFUL!! It also puts me into a deep sleep for about 3 hours. That's good too!! Ahhh…..sweet sleep! Sunday nights, I don't sleep well because I "fret" over tomorrow and "wish" there were no more!! With every treatment there is the good and the not-so-good, but thanks to my Father, completion is coming!

There is a song our church choir sings, "It's Only a Test". It says, "It's only a test we're going through, it'll be over very soon." I know God has always been beside me to see me through every test in life. Through tests of faith, I grow. Just like Job in the Old Testament, sometimes God "allows" tests of our faith to come. Some tests (like for Job), may bring us BACK to God, and some will make us stronger in our faith and some will teach us more of Him. God scolded Job for his pride and judgmental attitude, Job 40:2, *"Shall he that contendeth with God instruct Him"*? In verse 4, Job admitted his wrong doing, *"Behold, I am vile....I will lay my hand upon my mouth."* Then God told Job to save himself (vs. 6-7) God spoke to Job out of a whirlwind, He was saying, "stand tall", "", "get on with it", and "come back"! In 42:6 Job said, *"I abhor myself and repent in dust and ashes."* God knows how "impatient" I am. I'm that NOW person!! I want everything with the snap of the fingers. I don't like to be "slow", "weak", or "sick" and want my strength, like, not tomorrow, but TODAY! I catch myself wanting to say "Why" or "Why not NOW?"

I have to remind myself not to say "why", like Job, not to contend with God. God had a "divine diagnosis" for Jobs problem in life and in the end Job "Came Back" and acknowledged the greatness of God. Then! Job had more than he ever had before his trials! I acknowledge the greatness of God, the power of His healing hand and know He will bring me back to strength, health and long life that EXCEED that of the past and MORE than I could ever imagine! He has a Divine Prognosis for me!

Father, "I'm Back" at Your discretion, in Your arms and totally depending on You. Your love deserves my patience! Thank You for being a persevering God!

If I say, Surely the darkness shall cover me; even the night shall be light about me. Yea, the darkness hideth not from thee; but the night shineth as the day: the darkness and the light are both alike to thee. For thou hast possessed my reins thou hast covered me in my mother's womb.
Psalm 139:11-13

"The Third Leg of the Journey"

Daily Dose of Grace:
Stay on track, follow directions, keep God before you; travel the route with patience and expected delays

"And the Lord, he it is that doth go before thee; he will be with thee, he will not fail thee, neither forsake thee: fear not, neither be dismayed."
Deuteronomy 31:8

My husband (Sam) and I have always teased each other about "whom" (which of us) reads a map better! On vacation trips, most especially, I am usually the "navigator". We've discovered in these days that both of us have some map reading difficulties. One thing I DO pride myself in, I <u>WILL</u> STILL STOP AND ASK FOR DIRECTIONS!! (smile)

Yesterday, I discovered that apparently I don't "listen" to directions very well. It was my understanding, yesterday, "most likely" would be my LAST chemo treatment. I went into the clinic "feeling my oats" (HIGH ON HOPES) and I said to my favorite nurse, Hazel, *"Hazel! This is my LAST one, and I'll see the doctor next week, right?"* She said, *"No! We need to talk, come in my office!"* Uh-Oh!

Well......I found out, yesterday, was day one of cycle 3! Now I look back to the beginning of my journey, when I heard the doctor say "four"; and I think he must have said "four CYCLES". I have completed 2 cycles (4 treatments each) and now I've started cycle 3!! Oh well!! Now I suppose I need to quit saying, *"Are we there yet?"* and wait more patiently for the time the doctor says, *"We're there!"* My "socks were knocked off" (smile), not just in my "spirit" but also.....I know that was a new type of chemo. WHOP! I'm having difficulty "moving". I'm "shuffling" instead of my preferred "do-si-do"!

Sometimes a journey has multiple roads we must travel; some are smooth and wide and we can move in the fast lane and view glorious landscape and some roads are rough, and narrow and we must move in the slow lane with less appealing surroundings, but, it is still a road we must take to get there (to our destination).

I'm reminded of 3 men (of many) in the Bible who traveled some difficult roads to their destinations: Paul (ship wrecks), Jonah (in the belly of a whale - as Sam would say it "a whale of a trip!") and Moses (40 years of journeying in the wilderness).

O.K.! I must learn from them! If I can persevere (as Paul); go where God says, (despite the challenges) as Jonah and stay focused on the Promised Land as Moses; this will "soon" be a memorable "trip".

"Blindsided"

Daily Dose of Grace:
God gives hope that will help to overcome troublesome times

"These things I have spoken unto you, that in me ye might have peace. In the world ye shall have tribulation: but be of good cheer; I have overcome the world."
John 16:33

This has been a week of tragedy in America (The Virginia Tech Massacre). T.V. and Radio has been engulfed with continuous coverage as to the "who's" and the "why's" and prevention "if's". Many, many families (30+) are suffering with loss and dealing with a tragedy that "blindsided" them.
I have shed tears as I've watched interviews with families and friends of the victims. Truth is, we were ALL "blindsided"! We don't know "when" these things are coming! If we did, wouldn't we try to "prevent" them, to protect those in harms way? But!!! As the week progresses, I hear there WERE "signs of prevailing danger and then of some failed attempts of warning and lots of <u>disregard</u> or <u>ignorance</u> of the signs!

All of this is the way of the devil! As the Word says in Eccl.9:12, *"A man knoweth not his time......the sons of men are snared in an evil time, when it falleth suddenly upon them"*. ALWAYS, the devil *"walks about as a roaring lion, seeking whom he may devour"*. (I Peter 5:8). Satan is a "blind-sider", but **we have been warned**!

I think of David, as a young man, and how he was "blindsided" by King Saul, who turned against him because

113

he was so jealous of the attention David was getting as a great warrior. He (Saul) was out to kill David because he wasn't getting all the attention! Jonathan, Saul's son, and best friend to David, warned him of the danger and David was able to escape (I Samuel 19).

Well....the same story is true for us. Is there ever a good time for cancer? All through the Word we have warnings of the ways of Satan. The Word also gives us knowledge of ways to cope, to escape, to prevail! God loves us and gives us peace and hope to live in a troubled world and the promise of a new life in a new world (heaven) some day. Satan will be cast into the pit of hell, chained and we'll live in freedom and joy! There'll be no pain, no sickness, and no death! It's all a choice we must make.

It's good to know, when we are "blindsided", even if attacked by cancer; we can have peace, hope and courage along the way! God makes Himself known, standing with open arms to comfort us! **My God is holy** and always available when we are "Blindsided"!

"A Position of Liberty"

Daily Dose of Grace:
There is liberty in life and in death; EXPECT victory

"O, death, where is thy sting? O grave, where is thy victory? The sting of death is sin; and the strength of sin is the law. But Thanks be to God, which giveth us the victory through our Lord Jesus Christ."
I Corinthians 15:54-57

A spirit of sadness grips my heart today! My neighbor, "Fly", passed away this morning. The shock of the *"sting of death"* is always hurtful. He will be missed in our friendly neighborhood.

Everyone knew "Fly" and he knew everybody; always waving, taking time to talk and visit and a living example of fun and laughter. "Fly" and I have fought "together" over the past 6 months, compared our symptoms, shared the challenges and kept each other "lifted" in spirit. He fought hard, but lost his battle with lung cancer. As I have sat being sad this morning, God has reminded me of three things about death! 1) Death comes to all (sin brought it our way); 2) God has provided us with "liberty" to conquer, (through His Son Jesus) *"…….where the spirit of the Lord is, there is "liberty"* II Cor. 3:17; and 3) If we *"stand fast in the liberty of Christ"* (accept Him as Lord and Savior) He will *"make us free"* (liberate us); and *"we will not be entangled again with the yoke of bondage"* (Galatians 5:1). Cancer brought "bondage" to "Fly". But, today God has given him liberty and victory because he is in the arms of Jesus. *"…….Death is swallowed up in victory"*.

I Cor. 15:54. **My God is Wonderful!** TODAY! God put "Fly" in *"A Position of Liberty"*.

Today, my two year old granddaughter came by for a visit and as usual the first thing she says as she exits the truck is, *"Go say hi to "June"* (Junior, *alias* "Fly"). Her mother and I tell her "June" is no longer with us but that he has gone to heaven to live with Jesus. She will miss "Fly" and one day she will be old enough to understand how great God's love is and that the *"pain of death is swallowed up in victory"*. "Fly" is no longer bound by the pain of a terrible disease but is a heavenly, living example of God's grace and liberating power!

Thank you, Father for "A Position of Liberty" accessible to all who will believe.

"God of All Comfort"

Daily Dose of Grace:
You can expect God to comfort you, physically, mentally and spiritually

"But I would not have you to be ignorant, brethren, concerning them which are asleep, that ye sorrow not, even as others which have no hope. For if we believe that Jesus died and rose again, even so them also which sleep in Jesus will God bring with him."
I Thessalonians 8:13-14

This has been a tough week! I've not only dealt with physical strength but with "consoling" strength. My dear friend and neighbor, "Fly", succumbed to lung cancer. I searched for wisdom in the <u>consolation</u> of his family! I pleaded for <u>strength</u> to do what I needed to do!

I asked myself questions like; *"How will Fly's family think of me?"; "Will they say, 'Why him, not Donna?"; "It's not fair!"; "How can cancer be so discriminate?" "Wonder if she'll make it?"* or *"Will her journey be the same?"* Oh yes! I've even said to myself, *"How can I say I'm sorry, without feeling 'guilty' that I'm so blessed to be alive?"* These were tough questions!

On the evening of his death, Sam and I walked those L – O – N – G steps next door. Fly's son, Ray, embraced me and said, *"Ms. D, I've been avoiding you today!* I replied, *"Me too! I've been avoiding you!"* We hung on to each other and tears flowed. It didn't take a lot of words for us to "console" each other. We understood each others feelings. Consolation and

117

comfort DOESN'T have to be demonstrated in a lot of words. Consolation ability comes by total dependence on God, *"a very present help* (Psalm 46:1).

In searching the Scriptures for answers this week, I'm blessed to be reminded that *"God is the Father of all mercy and God of all comfort"* (II Cor. 1:3). He gives us "strength" when we need it, "words" when the time is right, and a "touch" when we're overcome with fear of what to say, how to say it and when to say it.

I love Paul's words in I Thess. 4:13, and then verse 18, *".....comfort one another with these words".* "Fly", my friend, was a child of God! Ray and I can rejoice in knowing that "where there is CHRIST, there is HOPE! We can picture "Fly" in perfect health, with no more pain, resting and at peace with Jesus! Should I be jealous, like I was because he kept all his hair? Well......maybe a little! After all..........he also beat me to heaven! God also comforts with "laughter". I hope you can smile and laugh because you too know the **God of comfort.**

"An Everywhere God!"

Daily Dose of Grace:
Believe in the ever presence of the One and Only, Infinitely Wise God

"Am I a God at hand, saith the Lord, and not a God afar off? Can any hide himself in secret places that I shall not see him? Saith the Lord, Do not I fill heaven and earth? Saith the Lord."
Jeremiah 23:23-24

The OMNIPOTENT, OMNISCIENT, OMNIPRESENCE of God just <u>blows</u> me away! So many times I've heard it said, "God is GREAT, God is GOOD and ALL THE TIME"! There's nothing greater than an OMNI-God in the days of cancer treatment and facing the "unknown". I am aware of the ever presence of a caring God.

Oh, my goodness!! In these months, I've really "hung out" with God. He has revealed more of Himself to me. I've always heard those OMNI words in church! NOW I FEEL THEM!!

My God is OMNIPOTENT – the One and Only, the I AM, Everlasting, Almighty, Jehovah, Creator and Preserver! (Gen. 17:1, Is 26:4) Some days He has been my One and Only always whispering *"I am"*, *"I'm forever"*, *"I'm your Preserver"*!

My God is OMNISCIENT – Wise! (Psalm 147:5, Daniel 2:20, Job 9:4) I trust in His <u>infinite wisdom</u> and rely on His guidance. "Father, there is no one like you! You know all!"

My God is OMNIPRESENT – Everywhere! *"Everywhere I Look, There is God"*! He is near me all the time!

I saw the movie, "Evan Almighty" on the weekend! It was a GREAT movie!   Not sac-religious or condemning of God's Word OR Christians! Parts of it "preached" good messages! In one part, Evan turned and God was riding in the car with him, he turned another time and God was in the office with him and another time and God was waiting under a shade tree for him! God was everywhere Evan turned! The point is, God IS everywhere, all the time!! Can you see Him?

Just the other day, Jo, a dear friend said to me, *"Donna, Camp Evergreen needs you! You have such a positive and uplifting spirit! Would you consider being a volunteer at Camp Evergreen?"* Camp Evergreen is a Hospice and Bridge-sponsored camp for families who are dealing with the process of grief in the loss of a loved one. I was AGHAST and HONORED! I responded to Jo's question with, *"Oh yes, I'd be delighted! I consider your invitation a God Thing!* WOW! How may I help some kids go through the grief process?   God is my Wisdom, He will provide!!   Then I remembered, John, Jo's husband. WOW!! The day after my diagnosis I was at the hospital for some more tests and ran into John in the waiting room. I told him of the diagnosis and he gave me a hug. That, again, was a God thing!! God put John there, that day, because He knew I needed a friend and a hug!

This morning, I attended the funeral service of my neighbor, "Fly". It was a difficult goodbye for me, but "Everywhere I looked, there was God!"   In the Scripture (Psalm 23) *"His goodness and mercy"*, it has followed me in days past and again today. Like the song "I need Thee, Oh, I need Thee, every hour I need Thee"; I needed God again today and He was there!

I will never "go through" anything alone! I praise You Father, jump for joy, clap my hands and say thank You!" **My God is OMNISCIENT, OMNI-PRESENT AND OMNIPOTENT!** He is my OMNI – GOD!

"Is This the Right Way?"

Daily Dose of Grace:
You can count on the wisdom and direction of God

"Lord, my heart is not haughty, nor mine eyes lofty: neither do I exercise myself in great matters, or in things too high for me."
Psalm 131:1

I remember one day I was looking for a new car dealership (my car needed serviced) and I couldn't find it! I thought I was going the right way and changed directions twice, fretting that I'd be late for my appointment, feeling foolish and wanting just to go back home. I was so upset I could not remember where it was! Then I breathed a prayer of desperation, *"Lord, just help me find this place, please!"* I found that after I prayed, calmness took over and I found the way! AMAZING!!! If I had just "Let go and let God, sooner, I'd have saved myself a lot of needless tension. I find myself "getting lost" in the expression of my independence sometimes. God "serves notice" and asks, *"Why don't you just LET GO and LET ME?"*

Today I found myself wondering, "Is this chemo REALLY the <u>right way</u>?" I had gone for a scheduled treatment and after lab work was told that my blood platelet count was too low and they couldn't do the treatment. Of course I didn't mind missing the "discomfort", but was concerned. Low platelets can be one of the side-affects of the chemo. Treat-

Treatment options are (possible blood transfusion and/or bone marrow transplant) if it becomes serious. The symptoms are easy bruising, bleeding, weakness and tiredness. I can definitely attest to the weak and tired over the past 2 weeks. Oh the consequences!

"Choices and consequences" are things to ponder! When I think of "choices", I think of right and wrong. Consequences equal outcome or pay-back.

Right, wrong and pay-back are lessons we taught our three children in their formative years. In Proverbs 2:6-9 and 4:10-27, Solomon laid it on the line and said it best. I cannot count the times that I have pointed out pieces of Proverbs to the kids, most especially our son. I've discovered over the years that the time may come when you just have to turn it all over to God, "Let go and let God"!

Chemo (the choice) really can cause (consequences) other health problems, so once again I ponder and weigh my options; consequences both good and bad!! I know what I must do; I just have to "let go and let God". I trust Him to steer me the right way.

Father, help me to turn off my frustration, my fear and my questions and trust in You! You are ALL WISE!

"A Life Well Remembered"

Daily Dose of Grace:
Your life in this journey can be an example of strength and inspiration to others

"For even hereunto were ye called: because Christ also suffered for us, leaving us an example, that ye should follow his steps:"
I Peter 2:21

If anything could be accomplished in this "journey" beyond my healing, I'd want it to be that in all things I would be remembered as an example (an inspiration) to others on this journey; that "seeds of faith" would sprout, hope for healing would be the gain and God's grace would be proven plenteous, prolific and profitable.

I remember reading the news article of an old automobile (classic) that a man had buried in a steel vault (time capsule) for preservation. After many years the vault was opened and expectations were high that the car would be in the mint condition of the day it was buried. What was revealed brought gasps of great disappointment to the crowd. The car was rubble, rust and decay; it would be an impossibility to restore. A car, hoped to be a "treasure", came back as "dust" and could NOW only be remembered! Above all, I hope people will remember me as an example of faith! Christ died and left me to be an example (I Peter 2:21). I pray my penned words will touch the lives of hundreds!

A dear family friend, Sam Y., sent this word to me, *"Your inspiration is strength perseverance, all while (like a mirror) reflecting up at Him who shines on you."* Sam and his wife have been CONSTANT in their contact and encouragement to us! I hope that people **do** see my life focused on Him and His reflection falling back on me would be *"an example of believers"*, I Tim. 4:12. My life cannot be preserved in a time capsule but can be in the hearts and minds of people!

"Indelible Marks of Exhibited Love"

Daily Dose of Grace:

A friend always loves, all the time

"My son, forget not my law; but let thine heart keep my commandments: For length of days, and long life, and peace, shall they add to thee. Let not mercy and truth forsake thee: bind them about thy neck; write them upon the table of thine heart:"
Proverbs 3:1-3

Over the past months I have been on the receiving end of genuine, heartfelt love. You know, the words "I love you" are just words. Genuine love is in the outward demonstration thereof. I have been saddened that some I considered friends have not put love in action. We just get TOO BUSY to love!

There are two acquaintances I have made since this journey began, that I had not known before. One new friend is Cindy. She works with my husband and has experienced breast cancer, herself. She has sent me some great books of inspiration, some cards, and "even" some scarves. Then there is another new friend, Carol who works with my daughter, Holly. She is a cancer survivor also, and sends me some of the VERY BEST prayers and words of encouragement via email!! I love these ladies, they know how to CARE! They understand the "experiences"!

Caring is defined by the "act"! In Proverbs it says *"Love and faithfulness should never leave us"*. God expects that of us and love and faithfulness *"should be written on the table of our heart"*!

127

Mother Teresa said, *"Kind words can be short and easy to speak, but their <u>echoes</u> are truly endless"*. What if God had just spoken, *"I love you"* and never sent His Son to the cross? God spoke it and it was so! **My God is Immutable!** My desire is to be the portrait of a caring heart!

Father, thank you for <u>exhibited love</u> that leaves <u>indelible marks</u> on my heart and for "reminders" to care at all times.

"Not only to Survive"

Daily Dose of Grace:
Always know God has a "purpose" and can use experiences good and bad to His glory

".......be thou an example of believers, in word, in conversation, in charity, in spirit, in faith, in purity."
I Timothy 4:12

God has purposely put "quietness" in my surroundings, in these days, so I can "hear" Him more! The many ways that He speaks and the things I hear, just WOW me! I've come to realize more every day how TOO BUSY I was in the work force. I had to pull away on private retreats which were wonderful, but not frequent enough. This current "retreat" keeps me in awe. His Word reveals so much, that perhaps busy-ness caused me to miss. Now my ultimate wish is to "Not only survive, but to.......not neglect the gifts that God has given me."

   As Paul instructed Timothy, (I Tim. 12: 6-16)..so should I be, 1) an example to believers (Vs. 12), 2) read much, exhort and teach (Vs. 13), 3) remember and use the gifts He has given me (Vs. 14), 4) give my whole self to meditation/contemplation so I can profit (grow) and others can see that in me (Vs. 15) and, 5) watch myself, heed the doctrine so I may endure and others will be aware of how I endure (Vs. 16).

   To make it simple, God shows me every day in many ways, He is not finished with me yet. I pursue writing in hopes that people who read will know who my #1 is! In my proposed book about my cancer experiences, (no title yet) I pray they will find renewed faith, hope and determination to persevere. In the book of my childhood "Back When", I hope people will reminisce, remember the joy and laugh much. In my Joy 2 U book, I want people to know there is always JOY in living a Godly life. Through my gifts in clowning, music, puppetry, and speaking I can bring needed smiles to those who otherwise may feel hopeless, helpless and unloved in hospitals, schools, nursing homes even community Bible Clubs. Through gifts of speaking and teaching, I can exhort, train up and disciple those who will also give much of themselves to the cause of Christ. At this moment of time He is not telling me to "get a job", He's showing me I "have a job"; "jobs" to do! I must exemplify GODLINESS! *"Bodily exercise, profits little, but Godliness is profitable in all things"* (I Tim 4:8).

Thank you Father for showing me that there remains many reasons for me to survive! I will "not ONLY survive but...........I will flourish!

I will praise thee; for I am fearfully and wonderfully made: marvelous are thy works; and that my soul knoweth right well. My substance was not hid from thee, when I was made in secret, and curiously wrought in the lowest parts of the earth.
Psalm 139:14-15

"Rolling With the Punches"

Daily Dose of Grace:
Think of chemotherapy as a GOOD punch

"I will say of the Lord, He is my refuge and my fortress: my God; in him will I trust. Surely he shall deliver thee from the snare of the fowler, and from the noisome pestilence. He shall cover thee with his feathers, and under his wings shat thou trust; his truth shall be thy shield and buckler."
Psalm 91:2-5

In cancer rehabilitation and treatments there are lots of punches along the way. There are the needle sticks, the shots, the I.V.'s (5-8 hr. increments), nausea, vomiting, muscle and joint pain, nerve tingling, nervousness, weakness, shortness of breath, fluid retention, risks of infection, anemia, weight loss, loss of appetite, immune system breakdown, chills, fever, etc.; the list could go on and on. If you have a good doctor you will know about the side affects to expect with the treatment path you choose. Depending on your "kind" of cancer and the "type" of treatment, the side-affects may vary. Psalm 91:2-5, helps me to "Roll With these Punches (side-affects)".

Some days I walk into the clinic at full speed, but some days I am very slow and Sam has to help me! Sometimes I hop in (like a rabbit) but may crawl out (like a turtle). (Smile). BUT!!! Though all of these "punches" are not FUN, they help me remember that with them comes hope! I don't "fear" losing this fight. The punches are essential! I came into this "fight" with my boxing gloves on, my upper-cut strong and victory in mind! A good fighter can "roll with the punches".

133

I think of Joseph (Genesis 37:18-28, 39:22, 41:38-43). He had rolled with some "punches", (cast into a pit by his brothers, sold as a slave, accused of adultery) but became an important leader in Egypt. I think of Paul and Silas (Acts 16:16-34) who were dealt the "prison punch", for doing God's work, but were miraculously freed by a God sent earthquake, and Peter (Acts 12:1-11) jailed by Herod to please the people and freed by an angel. God still had great things for these three preachers to accomplish. Then there was Daniel, Shadrach, Meshach and Abednego, (Daniel 3:16-25) who were thrown into the fiery furnace because they refused to bow to idols, and were loosed to walk out, without a mere scorch and people came to know the True God!

There are GOOD punches that make us stronger than we ever imagined! I thank God, daily, that He is involved in helping me to "Roll With the Punches" because *He covers me with His feathers, keeps me under His wings and is my Refuge, Strength, Shield and Buckler.* I will continue to the completion of treatments (Rolling With the Punches), because HEALING AND LONG LIFE is in sight!

"In the Eyes of a Child"

Daily Dose of Grace:
Your outward appearance may not be the same; always remember and embrace "whose" you are

"Even a child is known by his doings, whether his work be pure and whether it be right. The hearing ear, the seeing eye, the Lord hath made even both of them."

One of the things that bothers me the most in my journey to recovery is the loss of my hair. I remember worrying that the kids at church would be afraid of me and that my grandchildren may not recognize me (that I might even frighten them). In my eyes, a woman's bald head is a "fright" (smile). It would never be my choice of "style"! My mother said that I was born with a head full of hair, so this is definitely my first "bald" experience.

One day I was on the web-cam with my daughter, Kellee, and grandsons (ages 1 and 3), in Hawaii. She encouraged me to move closer to the camera so the boys could see me. I was reluctant but after some persuasion, I allowed Sam to zoom the camera in on me. Kellee said, *"Jack,* (he's the 3 year old) *come here and see Grammy"*. Jack came running, paused and with wide eyes said, *"The doctor took Grammy's hair!"* It wasn't the first time he had seen me, but the first CLOSE-UP so he could really see my bald head. I laughed so hard, I almost rolled out of my chair, as did his mother!

Oh the innocence, acceptance and cute perceptions of children! I suppose that over the weeks Jack had put two and two together in his little mind (hearing his mother and I talk about doctors, etc.) and had just "perceived" the doctor was to blame for the "no hair" effect! I think he'd "skin" the doctor for "skinning" Grammy's head if he could! Kellee reminded him that the doctor didn't "take" my hair! (Jack had just had some surgery the week before and Kellee was fearful that he might be afraid to go back to the doctor for fear that the doctor might take his hair).

I was just so worried that my grandkids would be afraid of me but it has never phased them! They still recognize my voice and my demeanor! Our 2 year old granddaughter, Keira, is so fascinated, she always says, *"Hat off, Grammy, Hat off"*. She likes to rub my head! (At least she's close enough for "hands on"! Jack and Joey can "only wonder"!) I have a couple of wigs, but I can't stand them; they "aren't me", plus they are HOT and ITCHY! I don't care about scarves, they aren't me either! I prefer ball caps and hats and sometimes going without either!

In the eyes of my grandchildren and other children, they SEE and KNOW I am the same grandmother and Children's Minister that I was. I will always sound the same, love the same and act the same. God knows my outward appearance may change even more in this journey, but He looks at my heart. "………*for the Lord seeth not as man seeth; for man looketh on the outward appearance, but the Lord looketh on the heart."* (I Samuel 16:7) May the *countenance* of my heart shine more than my bald head, all the time!

Thank You Lord for the "The Eyes of a Child"!

"Learning to Lean"

Daily Dose of Grace:
You can "lean" on God, He will bear your suffering

"That the "trial" of your faith....................though it be tried by fire, might be found unto praise and honour and glory at the appearing of Jesus."
I Peter 1:7

There has never and never will be a man without pain in this life! Trials come! Hurt comes! Challenges come! *"Life is not a bed or roses!"* With Jesus it is **bearable.** Thoughts that always cross my mind when I hear of anyone going through a trial are, *"Do they know the Lord? Do they know God is there?, Do they know He'll help them through?"*? I just can't "imagine" going through without God! I thank God, I can LEAN on Him! Has my faith been the GREATEST in the world? No!! But I have discovered that the MORE I LEAN on Him, the STRONGER I become and discomfort is easier to bear!! I believe that God grows our faith by "allowing" some trials to come. *"Knowing this, that the trying of your faith worketh patience.* (James 1:3)

The lame man in Acts 3 depended on the gifts "alms" of people for sustenance. From birth, he had been lame and DAILY he laid at the gate begging. God placed Peter and John in his presence for a purpose, "to show him where his "hope" was! The man "expected" alms but Peter said *"Look at me!"* Peter said, *"Silver and gold have I none, but such as I have give I thee, In the name of Jesus, rise up and walk!"* Peter and John could not give the man money, but they could give him

HOPE in healing, if he would believe in Jesus! His "leaning" on man, had to be laid aside and he was told to "lean" on Jesus. I'll bet Peter was thinking, "I can't allow this man sit at the gate, day in and day out, seeking alms and not know there's HEALING". Peter and John showed him how to "lean" the right direction! Once he re-focused, he was able to walk and leap!

This week I received word that another acquaintance of ours has been diagnosed with stage 3 lung cancer! His battle is just beginning but I know he'll "lean" on God every step of the way and I'm thankful to know of his Hope! I pray that my writings, my faith and my strength will encourage him!! NO! My God never wants us to suffer, to lack or to be sick but He does want us to GROW in faith, *know from whence our help comes*", and always LEAN on Him! **My God is Infinite!**

"The Music That I Make"

Daily Dose of Grace:
The music you make in life today, will live on in the minds and hearts of others

"Feed the flock of God which is among you......; Neither as being lords over God's Heritage but being examples to the flock."
I Peter 5:3-4

This week, I read about a physically challenged yet an accomplished violinist who, when playing before a phenomenal crowd of people, broke a string on his violin, in the midst of an orchestral piece. He KNEW he could not replace the string at such a critical point, and could not abandon the orchestra; through his expertise and determination he continued to play with a broken string, concentrating and improvising in such a way that the melody remained beautiful. The audience rose to their feet with applause. When asked how he had managed to hold it together and complete the piece so beautifully, his statement was, *"The task of an artist is to find out how much music he can make (play) with what he has left."* In other words, don't fret on what you lack but give what you've got and hope for the very best!

Some days my writing is challenged. I tease that chemo is "damaging my brain cells"! But, God always blesses me with re-assurance, gives me Scripture, the words and the art of putting it together (*"there are words that He can help me pen with all I have left that will be of benefit others"*).

Though my plans are to publish this writing to give courage, hope and strength to others along the journey of cancer recovery, God has given me opportunities to pass on excerpts to hurting and desperate people who are dealing with various situations. I hear God saying to me *"You don't have to wait until publication to help others"*. My goal in life is to be *"An example of believers, in word, in conversation, in charity (love), in spirit, in faith and in purity"* (II Tim 4:12) and to *"feed the flock"*.

A few weeks ago I received an email from Les, one of my #1 encouragers; he informed me that "one" he loved was just diagnosed with breast cancer. He said she needed encouragement and wanted to know if he could forward some of my regular email "updates" to her, to help build up her faith. I said, "Sure"!

This week I received an e-mail from a young man who had been a member of my youth group in years past. He said, *"Help me! Where is God?"* My heart "bled" for him and tears flowed when I read, *"You are the only one I can honestly say, I ever looked up to in church. You helped build my faith and I believed in God with all my soul and would have done anything, just to preach His Word; now I am a MESS!"* As I wept, God said, *"You've got some writings that will benefit him!"* It didn't take me long to respond!

If "The Music I Make" (my writings) NOW can help someone NOW; how much more is God going to bless the publication of this book? I must be the feet of Jesus in "The Music I Make"! *"Though I speak with the tongues of men and of angels, and have not charity (love), I am become as a sounding brass*

140

or a tinkling cymbal." I will *"play on"* with *"all that I have left"* and NOT *"abandon the orchestra"*.

"The Circle of Life"

Daily Dose of Grace:
Reminisce, laugh and be thankful

"Whereas ye know not what shall be on the morrow. For what is your life? It is even a vapour, that appeareth for a little time, and then vanisheth away. For that ye ought to say, If the Lord will, we shall live, and do this or that."
James 4:14-15

We (Sam and I) just celebrated our 40th wedding anniversary! Our daughters connived, planned and surprised us with a reception and invited many, many of our dear friends from over the years. It was great fun and a time to "remember and reminisce" of years gone by. We read, together, the beautiful words of so many cards and personal wishes and congratulations from friends and we "laughed" and shared about so many things of the past.

We've found that when the joy of years of a life together can be re-ran and remembered with laughter that is unceasing that it will always remain a "Circle of Life". I would wish that every person who has known us and each of our children and grandchildren will always remember the "circle" that we built. A circle knows no end and our laughter and love over the years will always be remembered with joy that goes on and on and on. The years have gone so swiftly by, *"as the morning fog"*. We never knew *"what would happen in the tomorrows"* of our life and we don't know *"the length of our lives"* but we do know that *"if the Lord wants us to, we shall live* and do this or that". If we keep God as the "center" of our lives, "The Circle of Life" will go on.

Laughter and memories sustain us. *"A cheerful heart does good like medicine, but a broken spirit makes one sick,* Proverbs 17:22 (NLB). During these months of cancer therapy, cheer and laughter have kept my spirits high. When I have a "down" day, all I need to do is "reminisce"! *"Teach us to number our days and recognize how few there are; help us to spend them as we should."* Psalm 90:12 (NLB).

Father, help me to "spend my days as I should", keeping you as the center of my life. I praise you for the memories, love and laughter and thank you for "The Circle of Life".

"God's Miracles, More than Instantaneous"

Daily Dose of Grace:
Take advantage of and believe in all possibilities for your healing, never limit the options that God will provide

"But without faith it is impossible to please him; for he that cometh to God must believe that he is, and that he is a rewarder of them that diligently seek him."
Hebrews 11:6

I remember early on, (after diagnosis and our choice of therapy) wondering, even worrying that some people might equate our choice of treatment as "spiritual weakness" or "disbelief in the miracle of healing" or even "lack of faith". I remember the story of Paul's healing of the lame man in Acts 14:8-10. Paul "beheld" the man from a distance and could see that he had "faith". He beckoned the man with a loud voice and said, *"Stand upright on thy feet. And he leaped and walked."* This man had never walked, he hung around and he waited for years, but never gave up "hope". God planned his healing on that day, in that way!

Simple faith in a healing God does not, in itself, eradicate the possibility of cancer returning to this earthly body, nor does it diminish my true faith in the miracles God can do. For example: I'm grateful for the invention of the light bulb, electricity and even the light switch, but without reaching for and flipping the switch, there will never be a sign of light. I have "light bulb faith"! Without my reaching for all possibilities and presuming healing, I won't know the outcome! <u>Faith is trusting God</u> and <u>presuming </u>He will do

145

what His Word promises, whether it is instant or a process. There is a fine line between faith and presumption. <u>To presume</u> is to say that God can and will only move (heal) in His own way and time.

God can perform the miracle of healing through medicine, science, technology and health professionals. I won't box God in to ONE way of healing (i.e. as the lame man) and exclude all other possibilities. I do believe that I am bathed in His anointing to be healed, in His time and however He desires. He is sovereign and free to heal in His way and time and I will take advantage of all avenues He provides. Faith is to claim His promise. God honors my faith, *"But, without faith it is impossible to please him; for he that cometh to God must believe that he is, and that he is a rewarder of them that diligently seek him."* (Heb. 11:6)

I have a positive attitude and hope for my healing. My faith and trust in God for His provision in His time and His way is my most "healthy" way to cope. I am not unspiritual or faithless because of the route I have taken. **My God is Miraculous!**

"My Church, My Cheerleader"

Daily Dose of Grace:
Your cheerleaders will give you a cheerful heart

"But be ye doers of the word, and not hearers only, deceiving your own selves. For if any be a hearer of the word, and not a doer, he is like unto a man beholding his natural face in a glass"
James 1:22-23

I have watched many a football games over the years and "know" that the cheerleaders play an important role in "stirring" the team to "fight" and the fans on the bleachers to "cheer"! The cheerleaders are the encouragers and the ball player's love being "cheered on"; it affects the game they play.

The battle I face with cancer is certainly not a game but I have a need for "encouragers"! I have high hope, a positive attitude and I seek God, daily, for strength. I walk every minute of the day in faith, trusting God, one moment at a time! Faith is my foundation but I can always use some cheerleaders! I believe that James 1:22-23 puts the responsibility of the church in a nutshell! The church has been given the power of God to be a ministering agent and the responsibility to be my cheerleader. Church members should be faithful to pray continually for a hedge of protection around me, to ward off the demonic realm that would seek to take my life! They should also encourage and "cheer" for the endurance of my family. I am blessed by two wonderful cheerleaders from an old church family (Margaret and Brenda) whose ministry is in sending cards. What a TRUE blessing those consistent and uplifting cards have been!

One day my body will give way to physical mortality whether it is at the age of 59, 89 or 102. God chooses! God will not short-change me, He'll cheer me on! I can rest in knowing that the number of my days are in God's hands; accepting that fact keeps me from self-pity. Through every quarter, (cycle of chemo) and every yard, (day) God will "cheer" me on to run for the touchdown, (healing).

My intention is to rightfully claim that those of "My Church" have also been "My Cheerleaders".

"Healing Rain"

Daily Dose of Grace:
God expects you play a "determinate" role in your return to good health

"Elias was a man subject to like passions as we are, and he prayed earnestly that it might not rain: and it rained not on the earth by the space of three years and six months. And he prayed again, and the heaven gave rain, and the earth brought forth her fruit.
James 5:17-18

"And the prayer of faith shall save the sick, and the Lord shall raise him up:....."
James 5:15a

I take great pride in my yard and my flowers. To me they are God's creation and my job is to "prune" them, to keep them beautiful. In the early spring the blooms came and my yard was like a "basket of blooms"! Then, a killer freeze came and zapped the blooms putting a screeching halt to the exuberance of spring.

Right before we left for our vacation things were starting to perk up again and I left thinking we'd return to a fully recuperated lawn. To my great discouragement, when we returned there was the beginning of a drought going on in Kentucky. The promising start of new leaves on my Weeping Mulberry Trees had vanished, the grass was becoming crisp instead of green; there needed to be some "Healing Rain" on the land. The signs were obvious! Pruning and added nourishment would be necessary but the pay-off would be forth-coming. IMAGINING the possibility, I was spurred to NOURISH the healing process. I was determined to "save" my yard, God's creation!

Yesterday, I had my 11th chemo treatment. Although I wasn't jumping hurdles or standing on my head, I was feeling decent! My nurse (the kindest and very best!) Hazel spotted me moving about the room, stretching my legs, and called me into her office! We had a lot of fun together and I guessed she just wanted to chit-chat. She looked me sternly in the eye and said, *"Donna, your labs are a mess! You have GOT to DRINK MORE water! If you don't we'll have you in here on IV's more than you'd like to know!"* OUCH! Just like the shock of the killer freeze and the drought, I was aghast to find out that my own body needed some pruning and nourishment (the signs were obvious). Typically, I drink only when I am "thirsty"; now I must drink even if I don't feel thirsty! Hazel has caused me to imagine the IMPOSSIBILITY if I don't start "pruning" more aggressively.

So, here I sit, today, consistently sipping on my water bottle and determined to pass the tests when I see Hazel next week! This water will be as "Healing Rain" to the blood in my body and I thank God for Hazel, for her caring and determination to make sure that I understand the part I must play and do what I need to do to get better! Here's cheers to Hazel and thanks to God for putting this important person in my life! I "drink up" with thankfulness! CHEERS!!

"God WOWS Me"

Daily Dose of Grace:
Look to a new morning, God is waiting to WOW you

"How excellent is thy loving-kindness, O God! Therefore the
children of men put their trust under the shadow of thy wings."
Psalm 36:7

I got up early this morning, not feeling 100%, but better!! I
"staggered" (literally) about the house, taking care of a few
chores. (I "stagger" on some days from the inebriated effect of
the chemo. Having never been drunk with alcohol, I would
presume that it is like unto this uncontrollable feeling!). I do
laugh sometimes, especially when Sam has to grab my arm to
keep me from "wandering" across the parking lot! In lieu of
self-pity I try to laugh, and can in so many of these
circumstances! Laughter IS good medicine!

I walked outside to our back deck and peered over the
railing. It was a beautiful day, just a glorious morning!
Suddenly the melody of "Oh What a Beautiful Morning"
started flowing from my mouth: *"Oh what a beautiful morning,*
oh what a beautiful day, I have a beautiful feeling, everything's
going my way". That was a GOD thing! My first instinct was
to say *"WOW God!"* God WOWED me with His presence. He
reassured me that *"everything IS going my way"*. God speaks
in such WOW ways!! THEN, my eyes caught the glimpse of
a beautiful new yellow rose by the pool! *"The earth is full of the*
goodness of God" (Psalm 33:5). It was such a bright "morning"
yellow and had a crisp "newness" to it!! I just "had" to go out
and cut it, and I placed it in a vase on my dining table! *"Thank*

151

you God for the rose!" Through it He reminded me that joy and healing WILL come in the morning and that a body weakened "for a moment" can be new again. *"The Lord is good, a strong hold in the day of trouble;"* (Nahum 1:7).

When I came back into the house my mind still kept working, WOW!! Then I thought! There has to be a great acronym for WOW that would be awesomely descriptive of God. There is! God is WATCHFUL (vigilant, attentive, guarding, protecting); God is OBLIGING (accommodating, helpful); God is WAITING (in attendance as a Lord in waiting). Now that is a WOW God!

I love the inebriated effect of an awesome God! He puts a dance in my feet and a song in my heart! *"O taste and see that the Lord is good:"* (Psalm 24:8).

Thank you God for always being watchful, obliging and waiting! Being constantly amazed (WOWED) by You, does not define me as faithless but even more hopeful with the sunrise of every new day! WOW God!!

"A Ride on the Wind"

Daily Dose of Grace:
God is the Wind beneath your wings

"For it is written, HE SHALL GIVE HIS ANGELS CHARGE OVER THEE, TO KEEP THEE: AND IN THEIR HANDS THEY SHALL BEAR THEE UP, LEST AT ANY TIME THOU DASH THY FOOT AGAINST A STONE."
Luke 4:10-11

I recall as a child, the "FUN" of flying a kite! First there was the wisdom of assembly, tying the right number of knots and adjusting the weight of the "tail" and of course the long length and durability of the string! Without the perfect tail the kite would take a spin (nose-dive) and the impact would cause irreparable damage. If the string wasn't durable enough, the power of the wind would break it and it would be carried away, out of control. If the string was too short, it would never reach the height of the "good" wind so it could take the indescribable flight! Then there was the "master" (the person holding the string) and setting the kite to flight. He/she had to be a fast and determined runner to get the kite started (to help it to "catch a ride on the wind", to promote the ascent). Then there was the navigator (pilot), diligent and watchful, guiding the kite with hands on the string; meeting the challenge to keep it HIGH and AWAY from the snares of trees and power lines, where it may never to be retrieved. And last but not least the navigator would be the one to bring the kite to a rewarding and safe descent, so the experience could be chalked up as an unforgettable journey.

Today I am sitting in the Oncology Clinic (a place I need to be) hooked to an I.V. I watch and observe as others, also, get their "fix"! My heart breaks for some I notice who are really declining in strength. When I see them, I say, *"I am TRULY blessed"*. I've seen them arrive for their first treatment, when their physical appearance was good and their hopes were high, and then in the progression of time, I see the inevitable changes, not only in their physical appearance but in their spirit. Chemo effects are tough to deal with, (sickness, weight loss, tiredness, slowness of mind and body, anxiety, sleeplessness, pale and sometimes yellow skin color, prone to infection and dehydration, loss of hair, gauntness and depression). It's a TOUGH journey! But when I remember God has angels *"in charge over me"* and they will *"hold me up"* over every *"stone"* along the way, it brings me REAL COMFORT! I describe it as *"Catching a Ride on the Wind"* and I pray that others, on the same journey, can come along for the ride. I can't DO what I use to, RIGHT NOW, but am determined to rely on God, He is my WIND! With Him always beside me, it can be the "ride" of a lifetime!

NOW the analogy of the kite to best describe the theme, "Catching a Ride on the Wind". 1) There is <u>wisdom of assembly</u> (the map or plan for the flight) – **knowing and understanding the treatment plan, its length and the prognosis.** Without a plan, life in itself, may nose-dive and be <u>irreparable.</u> 2) The <u>durability and length of the string</u> signifies my **strength and stamina.** If I can hang on to these, I can reach the height of the *"good wind"* and have the hope of exaltation to good health. 3) The doctor is the <u>master</u> and will be the <u>runner, fast</u> and <u>determined</u> to promote the <u>ascent</u> – **the journey** process. 3) GOD is my <u>wind;</u> with the assignment of His <u>navigators</u> (angels) they will GUIDE the journey <u>diligently</u>, keep me (the kite) from the <u>snares</u> (Psalm 91:3, 5) and bless my <u>ride on the wind</u> (Psalm 91:15-16).   4) When the time is right, He'll cover me with His wings and bring me to a <u>rewarding descent</u> - **end of therapy and healing.** (Psalm 91:4) and for all my days He will **hold me to remembrance** of an <u>unforgettable journey</u>. I will never take His healing for granted! My intentions are to always share the possibilities and the hope of such a journey with all who will read, listen and believe! I pray that they too, will *"Catch a Ride on the Wind!*

"Healing, Inside and Out"

Daily Dose of Grace:
God can heal the "physical" body and the body "spirit", You can count on it

"My bones are pierced in me in the night season: and my sinews (gnawing pains) take no rest. By the great force of my disease is my garment changed (disfigured): it bindeth me about as the collar of my coat."
Job 30:17-18

"Thou hast turned for me my mourning into dancing: thou hast put off my sackcloth, and girded me with gladness."
Psalm 30:11

A persistent companion in the process of healing has been pain. As the dosages of chemo infiltrate my body and barricade cancer cell production it also causes some extreme pain deep in the bones of my body, even to sore feet. This morning my day began with pain. I don't enjoy it but I understand it, I accept it and I endure it. With the tribulation of "pain", I hang on to hope and the joy of *"Healing, Inside and Out!* The Apostle Paul said it best, *".....but we glory in tribulations also, knowing that tribulation worketh patience: and patience, experience; and experience, hope:"* (Rom. 5:3-4)

I've learned a lot about the complexity of the human body and how it "works", over the past few months. Blood cells are produced in the marrow of the bones. Chemo affects the bone marrow (slowing the production of good blood cells as it purges the bad) and as the marrow works hard to reproduce good blood cells it causes pain. It makes sense! Pain is an element of appropriate healing. I recall in the early days following surgery, the exercising that was required to restore the flexibility and use of my left arm. These exercises were painful and extended over a 4 month period; but NOW I have full extension and use of my arm. Endurance paid off! Without the pain, there would have been no gain. Through the *"experience"*, I have regained *"hope"*! I am complacent in knowing that my *"mourning will turn into dancing"* in all aspects of this journey to recovery.

Just as I have learned about the complexity of the human body I have also learned and *"experienced"* the complexity of the human heart. As pain can come to the body, so pain can pierce and affect the heart (spirit). My father died five weeks after my mother, of a "broken heart". His "spirit" to survive, left him, when she died. Over 3 years of his own fight with cancer, mother had been his "spirit", his "will" to survive. Life isn't easy and the devil will throw anything at us, he can, to steal the spirit of survival.

Family *"issues of the heart"* have plagued me over the past few weeks. It has *"gnawed"* at me, *"bound me about as the collar of a coat"*. A woman is a woman for *"all seasons"*. Just because I'm "going through" this journey of healing, does not negate my responsibility to *"love"*. For me, it is now an experience of *"tough love"*, which I believe to be the only hope

for salvaging an otherwise always dependent, accusing and disrespectful connection. Tough love is a real heart issue! I have to strive to differentiate between *"heart **love**"* and *"heart **spirit**"*! Some days I "cry", not only because of physical pain, but because of heart pain caused by a wayward son. My nurse, Hazel, gave me a lotion for my feet, when I complained of the tenderness, and said, *"Here! Ask your husband to give you a good foot massage, every night, this will really help!"* Today, I need a good *"heart massage"* and I believe God will provide.

I am determined to pursue *"tough love"* with strength and honor, even if it hurts. I cling to the wisdom of Solomon in his description of a wise woman, *"Strength and honour are her clothing; and she shall rejoice in time to come"*. I believe *"tough love"* and endurance will pay-off! David explains it best in Psalm 66:10 and 12, *"For thou, O God, has proved us: thou has tried us, as silver is tried. Thou hast caused men to ride over our heads; we went through fire and through water: but thou brought us out into a wealthy place."* The days of *"tried and proven"* will pass, the *"sackcloth"* of heartache will be replaced by *"gladness"*. I rejoice in the promise and hope of *"Healing, Inside and Out!"*

Thank you, Father for PROMISES PROVEN BY FIRE!

"Maintaining a Will to Win"

Daily Dose of Grace:
Count the rainbows, believe in the pot of gold

"Fight the good fight of faith, lay hold on eternal life, whereunto thou art also called, and hast professed a good profession before many witnesses."
I Timothy 6:12

"Jesus said unto her, I am the resurrection, and the life: he that believeth in me, though he were dead yet shall he live: and whosever liveth and believeth in me shall never die. Believe thou this?"
John 11:25-26

God has been SO GOOD to me in this life. He's blessed me in so many ways and his blessings have given me the will to win, *"the faith to fight"*. Times like these cause me to reflect more on the blessings that fuel my will and that provide me with the power to press on. The Psalmist David says it in so many ways in Psalm 71, (I would call this a RAINBOW Psalm of WILL POWER and HOPE). David knew there wasn't anything He would ever have to face alone and throughout the chapter, reiterates that God is his Hope, Trust, Rock and Salvation. He said (vs. 5) *"For thou art my hope, O Lord God: thou art my trust from my youth."*

When I think of our beautiful grandchildren and dream of the years, yet, that I can enjoy with them; I consider them as coveted and lavishing RAINBOWS of "hope"! They are the rainbows that will lead to the "pot of gold" (healing). I will keep the faith, continue the fight and believe in the miracles of

God. I've been on the receiving end of miracles twice (healing from cancer in 1993 and a brain injury in 2004). Even the doctors say I am a walking miracle! Why would I ever choose not to believe?

I am "oppressed" when I hear of people in a battle that "give up"; perhaps it is my class-A personality. I wonder, *"Where is that faith, I thought they had? Would they give up so easily? Do they think it is God's will they let go? Do they have no reason to live? Do they have no hope of a future?"* Only Satan would take joy in one's "giving up". When Mary and Martha were oppressed with the death of their brother, Lazarus, Jesus reminded them, *"Thy brother shall rise again."* (John 11:23). I believe He can raise me to a life after cancer and that His will is that I pursue that hope for another miracle. I know God has miracles for all who will ONLY believe. When Jesus asked Mary and Martha, *"Doest thou believe?"* what do you think would have happened if they would have said, *"NO"*?

I am determined; I will not give Satan his pleasure but will be strong in my faith in a God who is greater. Only GOD will determine the time of my departure from this life, jut like He did with Lazarus and I can rest assured that I have a "hold" on eternal life with Him because He "bought" my way by the sacrifice of His only Son and I accepted that gift at the age of 16. That promise will not lose value if it takes me 50 more years to claim it and I'll go in God's good time! As David said, *"I am a wonder unto many, but thou art my strong refuge."* (vs. 7). I hope people can say that of me as I strive to be an example of a great faith! And again, as David said, *"Now also when I am old and greyheaded, O God, forsake me not; until I have shewed thy strength unto this generation, and thy power to every one that is to come."* (vs. 18). I will "Maintain a Will to Live" AND be an example to others on the journey! *"I will hope continually* (for another miracle) *and yet praise thee more and more"* (Psalm 71:14).

"A Reflection in the Rearview Mirror"

Daily Dose of Grace:
God can do more for you than you could ever dream

"Now unto him that is able to do exceeding abundantly above all that we ask or think, according to the power that worketh in us, Unto him be glory………"
Ephesians 3:20-21

This is an exciting day for me! My best friend (and encourager) drove me to my Doctors appointment. When I saw my doctor he gave me the good news; my blood work is back to normal and I will begin my LAST chemo-therapy cycle next week. This is Aug 6, 2007. I began this (chemo) journey on Feb 5th, 6 months ago. It is wonderful to know that the final cycle is here and that August 27th will be the last treatment. The headlights are on high beam and I'm seeing the end of the tunnel! Yes!! Chemo will be complete, it will become *"A Reflection in the Rearview Mirror"*, an experience never to be forgotten and IN THE PAST! I'm glad for this week, a "feel good" week, minus the chemo.

Doris (my friend) and I came out of the doctor's office laughing and dancing and thanking God. God has set my feet to dance and I exalt Him for seeing me near the completion of this battle (the tears and the pain) and for giving me deliverance, hope, victory and a future! No one could ever express love for the Lord, for what He has done, more appropriately than the Psalmist David (Psalm 116:1-9). In verses 8 and 9, he said, *"For thou hast delivered my soul from death, mine eyes from tears, and my feet from falling. I will walk before the Lord in the land of the living."* I would say, *"Ditto, David!"*

My hope is that every reflection seen in the rearview mirror of my life would be a reflection that would bring a blessing to someone. I want that reflection to be one of a great spirit and an enduring faith. I desire to be seen as a *"beacon on top of a mountain, and as an ensign (flag) on a hill"* (Isaiah 30:17), as having conquered a "mountain" and given God the glory!

As I write this chapter, I am speaking in present tense, but, in just a few weeks, this book will entail a "reflection" of a journey. I want its contents to be a **gift** of hope (*Daily Doses of Grace*) to another person in the battle for recovery. I desire it to be a **catalyst** of encouragement to family and friends whose calling will be to "applaud" along the way. And, I want it to be a revealing and dynamic **eye-opener** to those who have never, but may someday, travel the road to recovery. **I hope others may gain some eye opening ideas of ways they too can be cheerleaders!** With God it is possible! *"Now glory be to God, who by his mighty power at work within us is able to do far more than we would ever dare to ask or even dream of – infinitely beyond our highest prayers, desires, thoughts, or hopes."* (Eph. 3:20) I have always been **surrounded by His Grace.**

"*Fly*" September 2006

How precious also are thy thoughts unto me, O God! How great is the sum of them! If I should count them, they are more in number than the sand: when I awake, I am still with thee.
Psalm 139:17-18

"Matters of a Heart"

Daily Dose of Grace:
Speak your heart; sing it; write it; reveal the treasures within

"..........written not with ink, but with the Spirit of the living God; not in tables of stone, but in fleshy tables of the heart."
II Corinthians 3:3

If someone were to ask me today, *"Why do you write?"* my answer would inevitably be, *"Because of the **things**, the **occasions**, the **moments** and the **stuff** of (and in) my heart."* I have a dear and devoted friend (Carol) who encourages the writings of my heart. Her encouragement does my heart good and I write faster! I want people to "see" my heart. It is impossible for man to see inside my heart, but God has given me the ability to "pen" it so people can know those things, occasions, moments and stuff. And in these months there has been lots of <u>matter</u> in my heart! In the Old Testament, God told Habakkuk, who was fed up with the hardheartedness of his countrymen, who refused to change their ways, to *"Write the vision and make it plain upon tables, that he may run that readeth it"*. God said, *"...the vision is yet for an appointed time, but at the end it shall speak, and not lie:"* I must write the *"Matters of my Heart"* when God speaks to me, because now is the time and my great desire is that my writings will be plain and that all who read will be able to RUN! Paul said to the church in Corinth that their changed lives were *"as an epistle (book) written in the hearts of men"* (II Cor. 3:3) Heart messages are indestructible!

Again, when God anointed David as King over Israel, Samuel was surprised because David was a little guy, he didn't have the "appearance" of one who could be king. Samuel was sure that Eliab was the one God would choose. But, God said to Samuel, speaking of Eliab, *"Look not on his countenance, or on the height of his stature; because I have refused him: For the Lord seeth not as man seeth; for the man looketh on the outward appearance,"* and speaking of David, God said, *"but the Lord looketh on the heart."* I may not "look like" an author, but as God speaks, I write *"Matters of a Heart"*.

On the weekend, my doorbell rang and as I peeped through the hole on my door I could see Ray ("Fly", my neighbor's son) standing there. I opened the door and he stood there in such an arrogant and stately manner and with a big smile on his face! He said, *"Ms. D, I just had to come over here and show you something."* Slowly he rolled up the sleeve on his left arm and there was a masterful piece of art (tattoo) of "Fly". The tattoo artist did an explicit job, capturing the true likeness of "Fly" from an old photograph. Now it was etched on Ray's arm, never to be forgotten. Ray said, *"I had it put right here on my left arm, because that's where Dad's cancer first started"*. I came back with, *"Oh, that is SUPER, and it is also 'closest" to your heart."* Ray said, *"Yeah!"* ("Fly" passed away just a few weeks ago after his battle with lung cancer). Understand, that act was a *"Matter of the Heart"*. People cannot see "Fly" in Ray's heart, but he can always roll up his sleeve and say, *"Here's my Dad!"*

I never considered myself to be a "tattoo fan", and Ray's gesture has made me realize that when tattoos are *"Matters of the Heart"*, that makes them **most tolerable**. My son-in-law,

Steve, has tattoos of which he is very proud because they all reflect memories of duty assignments (he is in the Army), and family moments (date of his marriage and names and birthdates of his sons). They are all part of his heart. Now I'm thinking, perhaps I should get a tattoo that says "Survivor, God my Keeper", to memorialize this journey and this book! When people see it and say, *"Oh, what is this?"* I can tell them of all those *"Matters of a Heart"* recorded in *"God my Keeper – Joy in His Daily Doses of Grace"*. **My God is a Reminiscent God** who leaves indelible marks on the heart.

"He's A Keeper"

Daily Dose of Grace:
God is a Keeper of promises

"Be not afraid nor dismayed by reason of this great multitude; for the battle is not your's, but God's. Ye shall not need to fight in this battle: set yourselves, stand ye still , and see the salvation of the Lord with you, O Judah and Jerusalem: fear not, nor be dismayed; tomorrow go against them: for the Lord will be with you."
II Chronicles 20:15-17

God gave me a "keeper" of a husband! We've traveled lots of roads together in the journey of "marriage" and in this journey of healing. He has always been here for me! I remind our daughters of the "keepers" that their husbands are; Steve (Kellee's husband) helps with the cooking and the laundry and takes the boys to the park. Matthew (Holly's husband) is such a GREAT father to Keira! He also shares responsibilities of the household in every way! Both of these men are "keepers" for our girls and we are so thankful!

I am amazed at the many adjectives in the dictionary that define my God! "Some" of the "P's" I would choose are: Perfect, Personable, Provisional, Preserver, Powerful and Providential, and they are only a few. When I look at all the things, all the words that describe my God, I would sum it up and say, *"He's a Keeper"*!

Jehoshaphat, King of Israel, feared an attack of the Ammonites and Moabites on the children of Israel, and God said, *"The battle is not yours, set yourself, stand still and see"* (II Chronicles 20:17). God showed Jehoshaphat that He was a Keeper. The Psalmist David remembered God's protection in bringing the Israelites out of Egypt saying, *"Our soul is escaped as a bird out of the snare of the fowlers"* (Psalm 124:7). David remembered, God as a Keeper!

Through this difficult journey, God has been my Keeper! He has been my Encourager, Psalm 3:3, *"But thou, O Lord, art a shield for me; my glory, and the Lifter up of mine head."* In days of depression He has been nearby to lift me up, consistently reminding me of the promises in His Word, such as Psalm 9:9, *"The Lord also will be a refuge for the oppressed, a refuge in times of trouble"*; Psalm 50:15, *"Call upon me in the day of trouble: " I will deliver thee, and thou shalt glorify me."*; and Psalm 34:24, *"Though he fall, he shall not be utterly cast down: for the Lord upholdeth him with his hand"*.

God reminded me that the "battle" was NOT mine, was never mine and because I had faith I could "stand still" and "see". He has "delivered me", "picked me up" and "holds me in His hand". I've thrived on the premise of His Word. "The Lord is "on my side"! *"I will be glad and rejoice in thy mercy: for thou hast considered my trouble; thou hast known my soul in adversities; and hast not shut me up in the hand of the enemy...."* He's always been on my side! **He's a Keeper"**.

"New Life, New Beginning – A Journey of Purpose"

Daily Dose of Grace:
Wisdom is grasping faith, believing in mercy and accepting grace

"Now faith is the substance of things hoped for, the evidence of things not seen."
Hebrews 11:1

Today was the MOST significant day of my journey! This morning at 6:30 A.M. I "danced" into the Oncology Clinic for my FINAL (8 hour) chemo treatment. Seven months ago, I could have been as the Jew wandering in a *"solitary (desolate) way"* in the desert (Psalm 107:4). I didn't know "where" the journey would take me, but hung on to that wonderful reminder of God's greatness in Jeremiah 32:27, when God said to Jeremiah, *"Behold, I am the Lord, the God of all flesh, is there any thing too hard for me?"*

Faith, mercy and grace were my constant company! I am convinced that the human spirit plays a most important role in victory. The Psalmist David said in Psalm 107:1, *"O give thanks unto the Lord, for he is good, for his mercy endureth forever. Let the redeemed of the Lord say so, whom he hath redeemed from the hand of the enemy."* When the Apostle Paul spoke of *"finishing the course"* in II Tim. 4:7 he was talking about having "achieved" his purpose, (met his goal), which happened to be, preaching the Gospel and winning lost souls. **Faith**, *the substance of things hoped for* **WON** when Paul saw the *evidence*, the victory of people's lives being changed. I've finished the course of chemo therapy, *"a course"* God provided in the healing process. My healing is the *evidence*!   Today I give thanks; God's mercy and grace have been in abundance and He has brought me back, healed my body and rescued me from the hand of the enemy.   I prefer a **comeback** *to a* **fallback**! Pastor Jackson you can label me *"The Comeback Kid"* if you like (at least *"comeback"* is accurate)! God has brought me back to NEW LIFE, it has been a journey of purpose (healing and new beginning) and it is a wrap-up, victory has been won!

New life and new beginning have been such a perspective for me over these months. Ironically as I have been on the receiving end of new life to a diseased body, our daughter, Holly, has been waiting on the formation of a new life (baby boy) in her body. To correlate the two is such a neat concept. In just 3 weeks that new baby grandson will arrive. We will celebrate <u>NEW LIFE</u> in two ways in our family, the "coming" of a baby boy and the "coming back" of a grandmother! We will celebrate <u>NEW BEGINNINGS</u>! GOD IS SO GOOD!

In the next weeks and months I will pursue building body (physical) strength! As cancer treatment purges the bad cells from the body, it takes a toll on some of the good cells. That is the price that must be paid but with a spirit of <u>pursuance with a purpose</u>, that too will be temporary! I'll soon be back to running and am determined I'll be faster than ever. Call me the *"Comeback Kid"*, a person of ***<u>New Life and New Beginning</u>***.

Search me, O God, and know my heart: try me, and know my thoughts: And see if there be any wicked way in me, and lead me in the way everlasting.
Psalm 139:23-24

"Party Up! Party Down! Party On!"

Daily Dose of Grace:
God will be your Strength, Song and Salvation;
A most PERFECT Travel Companion

I was pushed back and about to fall, but the Lord helped me. The
Lord is my strength and my song; he has become my salvation.
Shouts of joy and victory resound in the tents of the righteous. The
Lord's right hand has done mighty things! The Lord's right hand is
lifted high; the Lord's right hand has done mighty things! I will not
die but live and will proclaim what the Lord has done.
Psalm 118:13-17

The troublesome and steep inclines, dangerous curves and bumpy road to recovery have been accomplished! Now comes post-cancer sustenance. I optimistically pursue the 5 year mark (the time when the doctor will say," you are cured") with the determination that cancer has forever been eradicated from my body. I believe I am HEALED!

By medical terminology I am now "in remission"! For the next 5 years I will remain under the vigilant scrutiny of my oncologist (an essential fare). I will take a daily pill; receive regular check-ups, blood work, etc. In comparison to chemo therapy I have said, "What's a pill? What's blood work? What's a check up? NO PROBLEM!" This week I have had CT Scans, X-rays and Ultra Sounds; been poked, pricked and indulged in those "delicious" radiology "cocktails"; and all to validate cancer remission. God knew how to get me where I am today and He knows methodical appraisal is pertinent and I will contend!

179

It is time to **_Party Up, Party Down, Party On_**, "....Quick! *Bring the best robe and put it on him. Put a ring on his finger and sandals on his feet. Bring the fattened calf and kill it. Let's have a feast and celebrate. For this son of mine was dead and is alive again; he was lost and is found. So they began to celebrate."* (Luke 15:22)

In just 19 more days I will celebrate another birthday! My twin brother, Danny, from Arkansas, will be here and we will celebrate together! We haven't "celebrated" a birthday together since we were 21 and in Germany! In 1994, he was here with me when I had my first cancer surgery (the week of my birthday), but there was NO party! Our oldest daughter and our grandsons will also be here from Arizona! It will be a birthday celebration to remember! Psalm 146:1-2, *"Praise the Lord, Praise the Lord, O my soul. I will praise the Lord all my life; I will sing praise to my God as long as I live."*

On Monday, I celebrated with and said "Thank you" to my doctor and nurses! Shouts of joy and victory resounded in the clinic, in the midst of other patients. (I pray they saw that there CAN be VICTORY.) While I am grateful for the professionalism, medical knowledge and kindness of the medical staff, they know *"Whose" hand I hold the <u>highest</u>*! They are excited about this book and I anticipate donating copies for patients in the clinic (one at every table, right next to the Gideon Bible), within every person's reach! Patients will know of the possibility of healing and be encouraged to hope and pursue; and if they've never picked up the Bible (God's Word); I believe that they will be drawn to it! My ultimate prayer is that at the times they may feel *"pushed back and about to fall"* that they will know *"from whence their help cometh"*

(Psalm 121:1). If that patient has never experienced grace before, I pray that *"joy"* will come in *"daily doses"*.

In the months to come I will chase after enduring strength. Inside I feel older; I move slower and my immune system is weaker; but, in time I'll be swift of feet and feel the strength as of Samson! STEP ASIDE! Some people have told me that I "look" younger (20 yrs.) on the outside! Praise God! I'll take it! I said to Sam (my husband), "Man! That means that for every chemo treatment I had, God made me 1 year and 3 months younger! Maybe I should do some more!" But he (Sam) could never control a 20 year old wife! God is SO GOOD! As I *"Party"*, *"I eagerly expect and hope that I in no way will be ashamed, but will have sufficient courage so that now as always Christ will be exalted in my body, whether by life or by death."* (Phil. 1:20) It is ALL for HIM!

"Father, I pray for the persons who may read this book; that You'll bless each one with COURAGE, FAITH, HOPE and "JOY in 'Your' Daily Doses of Grace". May each come to know "God as 'their' Keeper and "Party Up, Party Down, Party On"! Amen!

181

Printed in the United States
96595LV00002B/301-393/A

9 781603 830300